Praise for
It Didn't Start with You

One of The New York Times's 5 Books on Healing from Trauma, 2025
One of Oprah Daily's 10 Best Trauma Books of 2023
One of Book Riot's 9 Best Healing Books About Trauma for 2023
One of Healthline's 13 Best Mental Health Books of 2022
One of Cosmopolitan's 15 Books About Mental Health That Everyone Should Read
One of Men's Health's 20 Best Mental Health Books to Read in 2022
One of Choosing Therapy's 10 Best PTSD & Trauma Books for 2021
Winner of the 2016 Nautilus Book Award in Psychology
Finalist for the 2016 Books for a Better Life Award

"Mark Wolynn does a masterful job of illuminating the ways in which our ancestors' unresolved suffering, often unknown to us, disables us and binds us painfully to them. He gives us the tools and skills—an approach that combines understanding, imaginative dialogues, and compassionate reconnection—to free and heal ourselves."
—Dr James S. Gordon, author of *Unstuck: Your Guide to the Seven-Stage Journey Out of Depression*

"*It Didn't Start with You* takes us a big step forward, advancing the fields of trauma therapy, mindfulness applications, and human understanding. It is a bold, creative, and compassionate work."
—Sharon Salzberg, author of *Lovingkindness* and *Real Happiness*

"This groundbreaking book offers a compelling understanding of inherited trauma and fresh, powerful tools for relieving its suffering. Mark Wolynn is a wise and trustworthy guide on the journey toward healing."
—Dr Tara Brach, author of *Radical Acceptance* and *True Refuge*

"Mark elegantly weaves together the threads of generational and attachment trauma, offering a groundbreaking synthesis of neuroscience, psychology, and lived experience. Drawing on the latest epigenetic research, he provides a powerful *trauma language map*—a tool to help readers decode their symptoms, trace them to their origins, and begin the journey of healing. This book is full of healing sentences, practices, and rituals that guide readers toward greater awareness, integration, and repair. It is both a compassionate companion and a practical guide for anyone seeking to transform inherited pain into embodied wholeness."
—Dr Diane Poole Heller, author of *The Power of Attachment* and *Healing Your Attachment Wounds*

"Mark Wolynn's extraordinary book cracks the secret code of families and proves that you can go home again—once you understand how history made you. Full of life-changing stories, powerful insights, and practical tools for personal healing, *It Didn't Start with You* deserves a place on your bookshelf next to Alice Miller's *The Drama of the Gifted Child* and Dan Siegel's *The Developing Mind*. You'll never see your family the same way again."
—Mark Matousek, author of *Ethical Wisdom*

"Bridging both neuroscience and psychodynamic thinking, *It Didn't Start with You* provides the reader with a tremendously helpful toolbox of do-it-yourself clinical aids and provocative insights."
—Dr Jess P. Shatkin, vice chair for education at NYU Langone Medical Center's Child Study Center and author of *Child & Adolescent Mental Health*

"After reading *It Didn't Start with You*, I found myself immediately able to apply Mark Wolynn's techniques with my patients and saw incredible results, in a shorter time than with traditional psychotherapeutic techniques. I encourage you to read this book. It's truly cutting edge."
—Dr Alexanndra Kreps

"This book is essential reading. A must-read. Mark Wolynn's approach to inherited and early developmental family trauma and its effect on health and well-being is groundbreaking."
—Dr Bruce Hoffman, medical director, The Hoffman Centre for Integrative and Functional Medicine

"Utterly invaluable and endlessly fascinating, Mark Wolynn's book, *It Didn't Start with You*, links our psychology and biology in a profound new way, giving us the power to understand and transform ourselves in the face of what seems inevitable. Identifying our unconscious loyalties to our ancestor's trauma through a series of practical questions and exercises gives us the keys to unlock our own freedom and compassion. Reading this book is like being a part of one of Mark's transformative workshops, a brave and powerful journey to self-realization."
—Brenda Strong, Emmy-nominated actress (*Desperate Housewives, Dallas, 13 Reasons Why, Supergirl*) and CEO of Strong Yoga®4Women

"As medical doctors, we often treat the symptom. I've witnessed Mark identify the pattern and treat the cause."
—Dr Russell Kennedy, author of *Anxiety Rx*

PENGUIN LIFE

THE OFFICIAL IT DIDN'T START WITH YOU WORKBOOK

Mark Wolynn is the founder and director of the Family Constellation Institute. A sought-after lecturer, he has taught at hospitals, clinics, conferences, universities, and training centers around the world, including the University of Pittsburgh, John F. Kennedy University, Western Psychiatric Institute, Kripalu, the New York Open Center, the Omega Institute, 1440 Multiversity, and the California Institute of Integral Studies. Wolynn's articles have appeared in *Psychology Today*, *Elephant Journal*, *mindbodygreen*, and *PsychCentral*, and his poetry has been published in *The New Yorker*. His book, *It Didn't Start with You*, is an international bestseller and has been translated into 39 languages.

The Official It Didn't Start with You Workbook

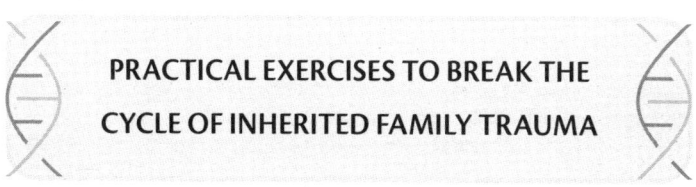

PRACTICAL EXERCISES TO BREAK THE
CYCLE OF INHERITED FAMILY TRAUMA

Mark Wolynn

Vermilion
LONDON

VERMILION

UK | USA | Canada | Ireland | Australia
India | New Zealand | South Africa

Vermilion is part of the Penguin Random House group of companies whose addresses can be found at global.penguinrandomhouse.com

Penguin Random House UK
One Embassy Gardens, 8 Viaduct Gardens, London SW11 7BW

penguin.co.uk
global.penguinrandomhouse.com

First published in the USA by Penguin Life in 2025
This edition first published in the UK by Vermilion in 2025

1

Copyright © Mark Wolynn 2025

The moral right of the author has been asserted.

Penguin Random House values and supports copyright. Copyright fuels creativity, encourages diverse voices, promotes freedom of expression and supports a vibrant culture. Thank you for purchasing an authorised edition of this book and for respecting intellectual property laws by not reproducing, scanning or distributing any part of it by any means without permission. You are supporting authors and enabling Penguin Random House to continue to publish books for everyone. No part of this book may be used or reproduced in any manner for the purpose of training artificial intelligence technologies or systems. In accordance with Article 4(3) of the DSM Directive 2019/790, Penguin Random House expressly reserves this work from the text and data mining exception.

Set in 11.5/15 pt Adobe Caslon Pro
Typeset by Six Red Marbles UK, Thetford, Norfolk

Printed and bound in Great Britain by Clays Ltd, Elcograf S.p.A.

The authorised representative in the EEA is Penguin Random House Ireland, Morrison Chambers, 32 Nassau Street, Dublin D02 YH68

A CIP catalogue record for this book is available from the British Library

ISBN 9781785045837

Penguin Random House is committed to a sustainable future for our business, our readers and our planet. This book is made from Forest Stewardship Council® certified paper.

CONTENTS

Author's Note   xi

INTRODUCTION Do You Have Inherited Family
              Trauma?   1
CHAPTER 1   How We Inherit the Effects of Trauma   15
CHAPTER 2   A Break in the Bond   25
CHAPTER 3   The Four Unconscious Themes   52
CHAPTER 4   Your Core Complaint   85
CHAPTER 5   Your Core Descriptors   102
CHAPTER 6   Your Core Sentence   116
CHAPTER 7   Your Core Trauma   132
CHAPTER 8   From Insight to Integration   152
CHAPTER 9   Reconnecting with Ourselves:
            Healing the Break in the Bond   168
CHAPTER 10 Reconnecting with Others: Healing
            Generational Trauma   180
CHAPTER 11 Rediscovering Connection in Your
            Relationships   211
CHAPTER 12 Maximizing Your Success   226
CHAPTER 13 Expanding Your Life Force   238

Glossary	247
Acknowledgments	249
Notes	252

AUTHOR'S NOTE

I've designed this workbook to be a guide to lead you through the rich landscape of self-discovery. You can use it on your own or work the material with a well-trained therapist.

Notice how you feel as you read these pages. If you feel agitated or anxious, a certain amount of that is normal. After all, we're excavating the depths of likely uncharted territory.

However, if you find that the intense feelings don't resolve, or you feel unsafe in any way with any of this material, it could mean you need more support. I suggest you bookmark the places that triggered you and seek the help of a somatically trained therapist, preferably one who's trained in working with attachment trauma.

Take good care of yourself as you read this workbook. Feel everything that comes up, as these feelings may be preparing the ground for the next level of healing that's arising.

The information in this workbook is not intended to take the place of a psychologist's care, nor is it a substitute for medical or mental health treatment. Instead, this workbook is a potent tool for unlimited self-discovery.

INTRODUCTION

DO YOU HAVE INHERITED FAMILY TRAUMA?

For the past thirty-plus years, I've been helping people work through the mysteries they live with.

Many of my clients have a symptom or behavior that doesn't make sense to them. It might be chronic pain, migraines, gut issues, skin conditions, or chronic fatigue. It might be depression, anxiety, or overwhelming thoughts and fears. It might be a relationship issue, a self-sabotaging behavior, or an inability to hold a job.

Many also have "ordinary" events in their family history: Their mom's or dad's parent died young. Their dad's little brother drowned. Their grandparents lost family members in war, during an epidemic, or in one of the many genocides throughout history. Their mother got divorced during pregnancy, lost a baby before they were born, or had postpartum depression.

Events like these, though they seem ordinary, can devastate a family. And because they are common, it's human nature to push down the emotions, to say, "What's past is past," and move on. But whatever emotions we push away never really go away. They often submerge in our body and reemerge as unexplained symptoms. And even if we're the one experiencing those symptoms, the emotions surrounding them, as we'll soon learn, might not be our own.

Substantial biological evidence has shown that the reaction to a trauma doesn't necessarily stop with the people who experienced it. The feelings and sensations—specifically the stress response, the way the genes express—can pass forward to the children and grandchildren, affecting them in a similar way even though they didn't personally experience the trauma.

This workbook will help you work with the mysteries *you* live with—the unexplained symptoms, the fears, the anxieties, the obsessive thoughts—symptoms you may think are yours, when in fact you merely inherited them from your mother or father or grandparent. And you've never made the connection—until now.

WHAT IS INHERITED FAMILY TRAUMA?

The latest scientific research tells us that the effects of trauma can pass from one generation to the next. Here's how it works:

Memories of trauma can become imprinted in our parents' and grandparents' sperm cells and egg cells. These changes in the DNA then pass forward to us. As a result, we can be born with altered brains that prepare us biologically to cope with traumas that are similar to the ones our parents or grandparents experienced.

Imagine the effect on your father if, as a little boy, he lost his mother and was placed in foster care. How would such events affect his ability to love, or trust others to care for him, or feel confident in himself? Not only would he carry emotional scars, but also biological scars in his DNA that can sift into succeeding generations.

Pain doesn't always dissolve on its own or diminish with time. Even if the person who suffered the original trauma has died—even if his or her story lies submerged in years of silence—fragments of life experience, memory, and body sensation can live on, as if reaching out from the past to find resolution in the minds and bodies of those living in the present.

THE IMPORTANCE OF ATTACHMENT TRAUMA

When there are multiple traumas in a family—or even just one—it can have a profound effect on a mother's ability to attune to her children. This can be particularly dire when a trauma limits the attention she can give to her child during the early stages of neurodevelopment. When this occurs, it can create a break in the attachment between them, disrupting the child's sense of safety and well-being.

There are myriad experiences that can break the mother-child bond. Maybe her partner cheated or drank and Mom felt trapped in the relationship. Or she had postpartum depression. Or she lost her parent or best friend when she was pregnant with us. Or a baby died before us and she feared we would die too. Or she had a trauma in her early history that affected her biology and psychology—and ultimately ours as well.

Attachment trauma can also be inherited. If our mother, father, grandmother, or grandfather experienced a break in the attachment with their mother, the effects of that break can epigenetically pass down to us. Whether it's attachment trauma or generational trauma we struggle with, this workbook will light the way for healing to happen.

IT CAN END WITH YOU

If you've read my book, *It Didn't Start with You*, you already know that the effects of trauma can echo in our words and speak through our symptoms. But our symptoms don't always resemble the original trauma. We may have issues with our eyesight, or experience tremors, but never connect these symptoms to the fact that our grandmother was orphaned as an infant and couldn't give our mother the love and attention she needed. And our mother, unaware of what she didn't get, couldn't supply us with the attunement we needed to live fully in our body, creating gaps in the way our nervous system functions.

As you're reading these words, you may be thinking about traumas in your own family or early life and wondering if you're being affected by them.

How do you know if you've experienced inherited family trauma? Here are some common signs:

- Fears or phobias, overwhelming or obsessive thoughts, and anxiety or panic attacks (though these last two are also common with attachment trauma)

- Unsettling emotions, such as a feeling of dread that something terrible will happen, or that you're a terrible person who could hurt someone, be hated, and won't deserve to live

- Physical experiences or symptoms that don't seem congruent with your life experience, whereas with attachment trauma, your symptoms could likely be traced to an early trauma of being physically or emotionally separated from your mother

And here are some signs of attachment trauma:

- Social anxiety, panic attacks, PTSD, trust issues, fears of intimacy, problems with boundaries, a negative self-image, and being emotionally avoidant or reactive

- Unsettling emotions, such as a feeling of being rejected or abandoned, ignored, or unworthy of love, being invisible, helpless, powerless, joyless, not being good enough, or being too much

- Physical experiences or symptoms congruent with an early trauma of being disconnected from a mother, such as food or environmental sensitivities, malabsorption of nutrients, eating disorders, autoimmune issues, chronic fatigue syndrome, substance abuse, as well as conditions related to physical touch such as fibromyalgia, eczema, rashes, and more

Of course, many of us have unexplained symptoms. Many of us grew up in a dysfunctional home or have parents or grandparents who couldn't give their love freely. How do we know if *we* have inherited family trauma or attachment trauma?

This workbook was created to help you find out. And not just to find out, but to heal, and break the cycle for future generations.

The effects of inherited family trauma didn't start with you, but they can end with you.

 **EXERCISE**

DO YOU HAVE UNRESOLVED TRAUMA?

Are you wondering if this work is for you? How do you know if you carry symptoms of trauma? Before we begin this work together, here's an opportunity to explore your own thoughts, feelings, and physical symptoms.

Let's start with a body scan. Beginning at the crown of your head, draw your awareness down the entire length of your body, noticing all sensations that get your attention. Where do you feel life force flowing? A sense of aliveness or vitality? Where you do feel the opposite—areas of your body that feel empty, hollow, numb, disappeared, or disconnected? Can you tell where the energy is moving as well as areas that feel constricted? Do some areas feel cool or warm, contracted, tight, or open?

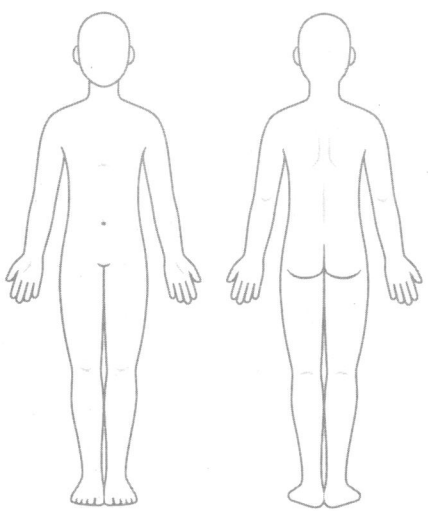

Whatever you feel or don't feel is fine. Let's mark it on the body map below.

Thank you for creating this body map. A physical image of what your body's feeling will be useful as we move forward in this workbook.

Don't worry if you're having trouble naming your physical sensations, or even if you can't feel anything at all. Just naming those areas as blocked, numb, disappeared, or disconnected is half the battle. *These* are feelings! And important feelings—ones you can work with. Having said that, I always advise working with a skilled, somatically oriented therapist if feelings come up that are overwhelming.

Some Physical Sensations Commonly Associated with Trauma Responses

- Fight responses: feeling tight, rigid, clenched, pain, an urge to attack or push something or someone away

- Flight responses: contracting, pulling or backing away, recoiling, panicking—a physical feeling of needing to flee or "get away" to create some distance between you and what feels threatening

- Freeze responses: a slowed heart rate; an inability to move or act; a feeling of being blocked, shut down, frozen, numb, hollow, empty, disappeared inside, disconnected, dissociated; going "offline"; going still or silent; flooding, sinking, or spinning inward

- Other responses that can be connected to any of the three: queasiness or nausea; shallow or rapid breathing; increased heart rate; feeling hot or flushed; sweating; trembling; feeling anxious, shaky, or jittery

Now let's explore some of your thoughts and feelings. On the lines provided after each question, please be specific about your experiences.

Do you experience anxiety? How does it show up?

....

....

....

Do you have depression? What does depression feel like for you?

....

....

....

Are there situations that trigger certain feelings, impulses, or behaviors in you, such as conflicts with others, being in groups, public speaking, or driving a car? Please explain.

....

....

....

In your relationships, do you have issues with getting close, trust, boundaries, or reactivity? Say more.

....

....

....

When you're close with someone, does it sometimes feel as though there's a glass wall between you and the other person? What does that feel like?

....

....

....

Do you have thoughts that distract you or keep you up at night? What are they?

....

....

....

Do you feel invisible, ignored, or unseen? Do you feel this in crowds, groups, or in your intimate relationships?

....
....
....

Do you have physical symptoms you can't explain? Say more.

....
....
....

If so, what fears come up as you think about them?

....
....
....

What might these feelings or symptoms be trying to tell you? What message could they have for you?

....
....
....

If you answered yes to even one of those questions, let's dive in and dig deeper.

But before we do that, just one more question:

What would healing look like for you? How would things be different in your life?

....

....

....

HOW TO USE THIS WORKBOOK

I've designed this workbook as if you were having a personal session with me. In it, I'll ask you all the questions I'd ask a client, and based on your responses, I'll suggest the same healing practices and rituals—just as if we were sitting face-to-face.

Here's a brief map of our journey together: In chapters 1 and 2, we'll explore the two different types of trauma covered in this workbook: *inherited family trauma* and *attachment trauma*. Then, in chapter 3, you'll explore the *four unconscious themes* that interrupt life's forward progress—four ways our relationships, success, vitality, and health can be disrupted.

The four unconscious themes are the gateway to the heart of our work together. Once you identify the main theme or themes that echo through your life, you can begin listening for your specific trauma language with the core language approach. In chapters 4, 5, 6, and 7, you'll identify your core complaint, core descriptors, core sentence, and core trauma.

Together, your unconscious theme(s) and your core language provide a map for healing. In chapters 8, 9, and 10, you'll learn personalized healing sentences, rituals, and practices to help you break the cycle of trauma. Finally, chapters 11 and 12 include special healing practices for healthy relationships and optimal success in life.

Throughout the workbook, you'll find both written and somatic (body-centered) exercises that walk you through the healing process one step at a time. These practices are designed to go deep. They may even hit a nerve or two. That's okay. I've discovered that lasting change often involves some level of discomfort. At the same time, remember you are fully in control of your experience. Whatever doesn't feel right, don't do. Trust your gut.

Although this work is yours to do, you won't be alone. Along the way, you'll meet two of my previous clients, Susan and Jordan,[1] who also experienced family trauma. They'll answer the same questions you'll answer, and you'll witness their stories of pain, mystery, courage, discovery, and ultimately healing.

For you to get maximum benefit from this experience, here are some suggestions:

- ▶ Set aside plenty of time and space for yourself to answer the questions and do the exercises. Be open. Be curious. Wrestle with them. Don't let them go until you've reached the depths. And then keep going. This workbook will guide you every step of the way.

▶ This workbook was created to support a number of different learning styles. You'll find conceptual information, real-life stories, open-ended written questions that engage both the mind and heart, and somatic exercises that engage the body. So feel free to use it in whatever way supports your healing journey: you can complete each exercise as you go, or read the entire workbook first and then come back to complete the exercises.

▶ Note: If at all possible, I recommend completing the exercises as you read the workbook. The power in doing the exercises as you go—not just reading them—is that you will be catapulted to the next level of healing, as each exercise builds exponentially upon the previous one.

As your guide, I will remain by your side as you enter a landscape of new discoveries. Each step of the way, I'll provide you with a tool that will function like a lantern, lighting the path forward. Let's get started.

CHAPTER 1

HOW WE INHERIT THE EFFECTS OF TRAUMA

Now that you have a sense of the journey ahead, let's begin by learning more about the two types of family trauma we'll be working with: inherited family trauma and attachment trauma. In the next two chapters, we'll take a deeper look at the science behind them and give you a chance to reflect on some of your own stories.

The history you share with your family begins before you are even conceived. In your earliest biological form, as an unfertilized egg, you already shared a cellular environment with your mother and grandmother. When your grandmother was five months pregnant with your mother, the precursor cell of the egg you developed from was already present in your mother's womb. This means that before your mother was even born, your mother, your grandmother, and the earliest traces of you were all in the same body—three generations sharing the same biological environment.[1] This isn't a new idea: embryology textbooks have told us as much for more than a century.

Your inception can be similarly traced in your paternal line. The precursor cells of the sperm you developed from were present in your father when he was a fetus in his mother's womb.[2]

There is, however, a significant biological difference in the evolution of the egg and sperm. Your father's sperm continued to multiply when he reached puberty, whereas your mother was born with her lifetime supply of eggs. So twelve to forty or so years later, one of those eggs, fertilized by your father's sperm, eventually developed into who you are today.

In either case, both precursor egg and sperm cells, science now tells us, can be imprinted by traumas with the potential to affect subsequent generations. Because your father's sperm continues to evolve throughout adolescence and adulthood, his sperm continues to be susceptible to traumatic imprints almost up until the point when you are conceived.[3]

With what we're now learning about the ways stress can be inherited, we can begin to map out how the biological residue of traumas your parents or grandparents experienced can be passed down, with far-reaching consequences. The implications of this are startlingly vast, as we see when we look at the emerging research.[4]

How Trauma Affects Our DNA

For stress responses to be transmitted to the next generations, the exposure to a trauma has to be "dramatic enough, long enough, and serious enough," says Isabelle Mansuy, a professor in neuroepigenetics at the University of Zurich.[5]

When a trauma happens, significant enough to alter our biology, information-rich molecules can latch onto our DNA and act like dimmer switches controlling which sections of the DNA get used and which do not—in other words, which genes get turned on and which get turned off. The sequence of the DNA itself doesn't change, but because of these epigenetic tags, its expression does. Research has shown that epigenetic tags can account for differences in how we regulate stress later in life.[6]

As a result, our behavior—how we respond in certain situations—can change. So can the behavior of our children and grandchildren, who can be born with altered brains and hypervigilant nervous systems preparing them to deal with traumas they might never experience.

Scientists used to believe that the effects of stress were erased in the precursor sperm and egg cells (soon after fertilization occurs) before any epigenetic information could affect the next generation—like data being erased from a computer's hard drive. Scientists have now demonstrated, however, that certain epigenetic tags escape this reprogramming process and are in fact transmitted to the precursor egg and sperm cells that will one day become us.[7]

If your parents experienced a trauma significant enough to alter the function of their genes, that genetic information, transmitted in your father's sperm cell or in your mother's egg cell, could predispose you to be sensitive or reactive to situations that took place before you were even born. Situations you know nothing about.

The upside is that you'd now have a better chance of surviving those situations. The downside is that your autonomic nervous system could remain switched on, stuck in sympathetic mode, even when no danger is present. Once activated, the nervous system often can't tell the difference between an unsafe past and a safe present.

If, for example, our parents or grandparents lived in a war-torn environment (with people being shot, bombs going off, uniformed men lining people up in the square, or loved ones being taken away), they could develop and pass forward a skill set—sharper reflexes, quicker reaction times—reactions to the violence to help *us* survive the trauma *they* experienced. The problem is we could also inherit a stress response with the dials set to ten, preparing us to survive a catastrophe that never arrives. And we rarely make the connection that our anxiety, our hypervigilance, or our depression is linked to our parents or grandparents. We just think we're wired this way, when actually, epigenetic tags have attached to our DNA and communicated to the cells to either activate or silence specific genes, often leading to fears, feelings, and symptoms we can't explain.

 **EXERCISE**

SHAKING THE FAMILY TREE

If you or one of your children struggle with unexplained symptoms—depression, anxiety, OCD, a phobia, a destructive behavior—it's time to shake the family tree and see what falls out.

Think back. What family secrets have been hidden? Whose stories didn't get told? What traumas never healed all the way? What story did you hear only once and then was never mentioned again?

What happened to your mother, your father, your grandmothers, or your grandfathers when they were small, or when they struck out into the world, or in their relationships? What disappointments, losses, or griefs did they experience?

....
....
....
....
....

If nothing comes to mind, here are some possible traumas that could be passed down to you and your children, affecting your relationships, success, health, or well-being. This isn't a complete list, but it will give you a good idea of the kinds of traumas that can impact a family for generations.

- Did a parent or grandparent lose a child, sibling, parent, great love, or significant partner?
- Did a grandparent struggle with depression when your mother or father was small?
- Did a parent or grandparent grow up in a war-torn country?
- Did a parent or grandparent have to leave their home or a family member they cared about?
- Did your father or grandfather secretly start another family?
- Was a parent or grandparent harsh, cold, distant, unfaithful, or an addict or alcoholic?
- Did one of your parents or grandparents die young?
- Did one of your parents or grandparents experience a separation from their mother when they were small?
- Was one of your parents' or grandparents' marriages empty or loveless?

Did this list jog your memory? On the lines below, write down something that may have disrupted the flow of love in your family.

....

....

....

Can you feel the echoes of this trauma in your own life? What fears, symptoms, thoughts, or behaviors may be connected to it?

....
....
....

Do aspects of this trauma reverberate in the lives of your children?

....
....
....

The more we know about these traumas, and the more we talk about them, the more we're able to bring relief to our children and to their children, who could be suffering without a clue as to why. I've found that when we ignore the past, it can come back to haunt us. Yet when we explore it, we don't have to repeat it. We can break these destructive patterns so they're not passed down to future generations.

When I work with families in my practice, I often see recurring patterns of illness, depression, anxiety, relationship struggles, and financial hardship, and always feel compelled to look deeper. What unexplored event in a previous generation drives the behavior of the man who loses all his money in the stock market, or the woman who chooses to be intimate only with married men? How have their genetic inheritances been influenced? What happened in their family history? What trauma was powerful enough to change their biology?

Researchers, for example, studied the children of genocide survivors—from Rwanda, Cambodia, and the Holocaust, just to name a few—and they found epigenetic changes linked to PTSD, even though the children hadn't experienced the original trauma.[8]

A 2018 study from Tufts University found that men who suffered trauma as children were able to pass anxiety to their children through their sperm. This particular study focused on sperm donors who reported having significant adverse childhood experiences (ACEs). The higher the men's ACE score, the more likely they were to have altered RNA profiles in their sperm.[9]

In a 2017 study published in *JAMA Psychiatry*, researchers followed mothers who suffered trauma as children and found that their daughters were more likely to struggle with depression and bipolar disorder.[10]

These studies show us why it's important for us to ask our parents, if they're still alive, what happened to them *and* what happened to their parents. The more we know, the more we can make sense of the fears, behaviors, and sensations we can't explain.

Ultimately, traumas from any event significant enough to disrupt the emotional equilibrium in our family—a war, a crime, a suicide, an early death, a sudden or unexpected loss—can lead to our reliving trauma symptoms from the past.

Given that transgenerational epigenetic inheritance is a relatively new field, and a generation in humans is approximately twenty years, we don't yet know the effects our traumas will have on our grandchildren and great-grandchildren. The results are still pending. However, with research demonstrating that stress can be transmitted for up to five generations in mice (and there's even a study showing more than three hundred generations in worms!),[11] it's important to not only tell our children what happened to us, but also what happened to our parents and grandparents. And if we know the stories, even beyond that.

THE GOOD NEWS

Up to this point, I feel that I've only given you the bad news—that we're all in the same boat, and it's sinking. There's actually good news. A lot of good news.

Researchers are now able to reverse trauma symptoms in mice. And the implications are vast, as mice share a strikingly similar genetic blueprint with humans—over 90 percent of the genes in humans have counterparts in mice.

In multiple studies, mouse pups that were separated from their mothers exhibited behaviors similar to what we call *depression* in humans. The symptoms seemed to worsen as the mice aged. Not only that, but the depressive behaviors could be observed for three or more generations.

Yet when those same traumatized mice are exposed to positive experiences, not only do their trauma symptoms disappear and their behaviors improve, but they also experience changes in the way their DNA expresses, preventing symptoms from being transmitted to the next generation. What this research is bringing to light is truly groundbreaking. Mice, after having positive experiences, are able to shed old trauma patterns.

Mice aren't the only ones who benefit from having positive experiences. It's also how we, as humans, break the cycle of inherited family trauma.

As you read further, you'll learn how. But first, let's take a look at another type of trauma we can experience—a trauma that occurs when our early connection with our mother has been broken.

CHAPTER 2

A BREAK IN THE BOND

"There is no influence so powerful as that of the mother," said Sarah Josepha Hale in 1829.[1] Our mother establishes the essential blueprint for how our lives will unfold. This unfolding begins in the womb and takes shape even before we are born. During this time, our mother is our whole world, and once we're born, her touch, her gaze, her voice, and her smell are our contact with life itself. When this bond is broken—either in utero or during the first few years of life—it manifests as one of life's most pervasive and frequently overlooked traumas.

While we are too small to make sense of life on our own, our mother reflects our experiences back to us in doses we can ingest and assimilate. Her ability to see us, know us, and soothe us—and the bond that creates—characterizes what is known as *attunement*. In an ideal world, when we cry, her face shows concern. When we laugh, she beams with delight, mirroring our every expression. When our mother is in tune with us, she infuses us with a sense of safety, worth, and belonging through the tenderness of her touch, the warmth of her skin, the constancy of her attention, and even the sweetness of her smile. She fills us up with all her "good stuff" and, in response, we develop a reservoir of "good stuff" inside.

In our earliest years, we need to acquire enough "good stuff" in our reservoir to trust that life will turn out okay, even if there are interruptions that knock us off track. When we get little or none of the "good stuff" from our mother, it can be hard to trust life at all.

On many levels, the images we hold of "mother" and "life" are interrelated. Ideally, a mother nurtures us and makes sure that we are safe. She comforts us and gives us what we need to survive when we are too small to give it to ourselves. After repeated experiences of getting enough of what we need from her, we learn that we can also give ourselves what we need. In essence, we feel that we are "enough" to give ourselves "enough." Life, in collusion, then seems to bring us what we need. When the connection with our mother flows freely, good health, money, success, and love can also seem to flow our way.

When the early bond with our mother is interrupted, however, a dark cloud of fear, scarcity, and distrust can become our default. Whether this break in the bond is permanent, as with an adoption, or whether it's a temporary break that wasn't fully restored, the gap between mother and child can become a breeding ground for many of life's struggles.

When the break is only temporary, it is important that our mother stay stable, present, and welcoming during our return from separation. The experience of losing her can be so devastating that we may be hesitant or resistant to reconnect with her. If she is unable to tolerate our hesitation, or if she interprets our reticence as a rejection, she might react by distancing from us, thus leaving our bond bruised and broken. She might never understand why she feels disconnected from us, and dwell in feelings of self-doubt, disappointment, and insecurity in her ability to mother us—or worse, irritability and anger toward us. A rift that doesn't heal can shake the foundation of our future relationships.

An essential feature of these early experiences is that they are not retrievable in our memory banks. During gestation, infancy, and early childhood, our brain is not equipped to put our experiences into story form so that they can be made into memories. Without the memories, our unfulfilled longings can play out unconsciously as urges, cravings, and yearnings that we seek to satisfy through our next job, our next holiday, our next glass of wine, and even our next partner. In a similar vein, the fear and anxiety from a break in the attachment can distort our reality, making difficult and uncomfortable situations feel catastrophic and life-threatening.

How Attachment Trauma Happens

Attachment experts teach us that a mother's bond with her child ideally begins at conception. How our mother bonds with us in the womb is instrumental in the development of our neural circuitry, and the first two to three years outside the womb function as a continuation of that neural development. Which neural circuits remain, which are discarded, and how the remaining circuits are organized depend on how an infant experiences and interacts with the mother. It's through these early interactions that a child establishes a blueprint for managing emotions, thoughts, and behaviors.

It's also during this time that we're developing a brain designed for safety and security, openness and vulnerability—or one designed for self-protection, defensiveness, and hypervigilance. Studies show that children who are exposed to unsafe and unpredictable caregiving—between birth and twenty-four months—can experience lasting and severe behavioral and neurodevelopmental effects.[2]

Our mother's ability to attune to us during this sensitive period, her ability to intuit what we need and comfort us, is a crucial component of this process. Basically, she installs the software for our well-being, or lack of well-being.

When a mother carries inherited trauma, or has experienced a traumatic event, such as a break in the bond with her own mother, it can increase the likelihood of an interruption in the tender bond that's forming with her infant. The impact of an early break in the mother-child bond—an extended hospital stay, an ill-timed vacation, a long-term separation—can be devastating for the infant. The deep, embodied familiarity of the mother's smell, feel, touch, sound, and taste—everything the child has come to know and depend on—is suddenly gone.

"Mother and offspring live in a biological state that has much in common with addiction," says behavior science writer Winifred Gallagher. "When they are parted, the infant does not just miss its mother. It experiences a physical and psychological withdrawal not unlike the plight of a heroin addict who goes cold turkey."[3] This analogy helps to explain why all newborn mammals, including humans, protest with such vigor when they're separated from their mothers. From an infant's perspective, a separation from the mother can be felt as life-threatening.[4] You can read more about the research on attachment trauma, with both mice and humans, in part 1 of *It Didn't Start with You*.

THE TURBULENT WOMB

We may know the story of what happened to us before, during, or after our birth—but it's rare that we have any cognitive memories from that time. More likely, somatic memories formed during that period remain embedded in our body, often creating a morass of confusing or unsettling feelings.

Chances are, if our mother was stressed, we marinated in a womb aswirl with cortisol and other chemicals driven by her turbulent emotions. What was she feeling back then? What was she telling herself? Was she pregnant out of wedlock? Was she frightened? Was she feeling ashamed? Was she feeling alone? Did she have the support of our father or was she feeling rejected by him? Did she even want to be with him? Did she have the support of her parents? Did she have to leave school, or leave her home? Did she have to quit her job? Did she have to put her dreams on hold?

We were there. Maybe not cognizant, but we were somatically aware of the changing experiences in her womb. What was happening to her was also happening to us.

The science of embryology supports this. Our physical heart forms within the first few weeks of pregnancy, as does the neural tube and neural groove—that which will become our nervous system. With a beating heart and the foundations of a nervous system, we were aware of our surroundings, on some level, experiencing the chaotic world around us.

Our mother's world—her fears, her thoughts, her feelings—was our world too. For any of us whose mothers went through a difficult time while she was pregnant with us, we'd experience her distress as a trauma.

For example, if she was considering an abortion or was planning to give us away, we would have felt the energy of the thought: "I can't keep you." We would have felt her turbulent emotions. Her anger, her shame, her frustration—they would have played a part in forming us. It's possible the remnants of these emotions could still be living inside our body.

For that reason, we need to pay special attention to how our body responds in our relationships, particularly with a romantic partner. Our early relationship with our mother forms the template for our intimate relationships. Do we trust easily? Do we feel supported? How are we still creating situations in which we feel abandoned or rejected?

The support our mother receives from her partner during her pregnancy with us is also critical to our development. If our mother was struggling in her relationship with our father, dealing with his (or her own) addictions, suspicious of infidelities, worrying about money, unsure of where she was going to live, concerned about how she was going to keep herself and us safe—all of this could create a traumatic womb experience, the effects of which can last for generations.

A turbulent womb often produces a hypervigilant, overly anxious fetus who's already learning epigenetically to adapt to stress by creating strategies to avoid feeling pain. Not only are these strategies forged in the womb, but they continue to develop throughout infancy and childhood.

How might you still be creating strategies to avoid pain in your life today?

Here are some common strategies we employ to avoid pain, seek attention, avoid attention, or similarly control our environment.

I become:

- ☐ efficient
- ☐ capable
- ☐ uber intelligent
- ☐ self-sufficient
- ☐ hyper-independent
- ☐ agreeable
- ☐ a people pleaser
- ☐ a giver
- ☐ a caretaker
- ☐ conflict avoidant
- ☐ aggressive
- ☐ controlling
- ☐ self-aggrandizing
- ☐ invisible

How might these strategies be affecting your relationships? Your career? Your health? Your vitality?

....

....

....

In the chart below, list some of the strategies you have created and their effects on your life, career, health, relationships, and other areas important to you.

STRATEGY	EFFECT ON CAREER	EFFECT ON RELATIONSHIP	EFFECT ON HEALTH	EFFECT ON	EFFECT ON

For each of the strategies you identified above, now think about the people you use them with, the behaviors you notice in yourself, and what you lose by being this way (for example, I lose energy, boundaries, authenticity, connection with others).

STRATEGY	PEOPLE	BEHAVIORS	WHAT I LOSE

If we experienced difficulties during gestation or birth, or, as an infant, lapses in our mother's care or attention, all is not lost. Fortunately, a broken bond with our mother can heal at any time in our lives.

Healing the break is primarily about reconnecting with ourselves—with that child part of us who felt alone and uncared for, or who told us we needed to be strong, efficient, and self-sufficient to survive.

TYPES OF SEPARATIONS THAT CREATE A BREAK IN THE BOND

Although the vast majority of women approach motherhood with the best of intentions, situations beyond a mother's control can lead to early separations from her child. Some of these separations are physical in nature. In addition to adoption, events that involve an extended period of separation, such as birth complications (a fetus being asphyxiated by the umbilical cord, enduring a protracted labor, being in an incubator, or a mother or child in medical distress), hospitalizations and illnesses, work trips, or vacations, can all threaten the developing bond.

Are you aware of any physical separations you may have had from your mother when you were young? If so, what happened?

....

....

....

....

....

Emotional disconnections function similarly. As children, we need our mother's emotional and energetic presence as much as we need her physical presence. When the mother is physically available, but her focus and attention are sporadic, the child does not feel safe and secure. When our mother experiences a traumatic event—such as the loss of a pregnancy, a child, a parent, a partner, a home, her health—her attention can be pulled away from us. We, in turn, experience the trauma of losing her. Or if our mother was emotionally flatlined or too matter-of-fact, unable to match the energy behind our emotions—our exuberance, our terror, our pain—such a disconnect between our experience and her mirroring can break the fragile bond that's forming between us.

Are you aware of any emotional disconnections you may have had from your mother when you were young? If so, say more.

....
....
....
....
....

Disconnections between mother and child, as we just learned, can also occur in the womb. High levels of fear, anxiety, or depression; a stressful relationship with a partner; the death of a loved one; a negative attitude about being pregnant; a previous loss in utero; or a fear of losing the pregnancy can all interrupt a mother's attunement with her developing baby.

Based on what you know, describe what was going on with your mother during her pregnancy with you (especially any fear, anxiety, depression, stress, etc.).

....
....
....
....
....

Disconnections can also be inherited. Mothers often pass on the mothering that they themselves received. If our mother experienced a break in the bond with her mother, that trauma can filter, to some degree, into the mothering she's able to give. Even if our mother was able to give us the type of care we needed, we could still inherit the effects of her break in the bond through her egg—or the effects of our father's break in the bond through his sperm. We could relive their fears, their terrors, their anxieties, and experience their fight, flight, freeze responses as though they were our own. And if we look back another generation or two, we might discover that breaks in the mother-child bond existed there too.

In the diagram on the next page, next to "your grandmother," list the traumas your grandmother experienced (as a fetus, infant, toddler, or small child, if you know them) that may have affected her attachment with her mother. Do the same for your mother and yourself.

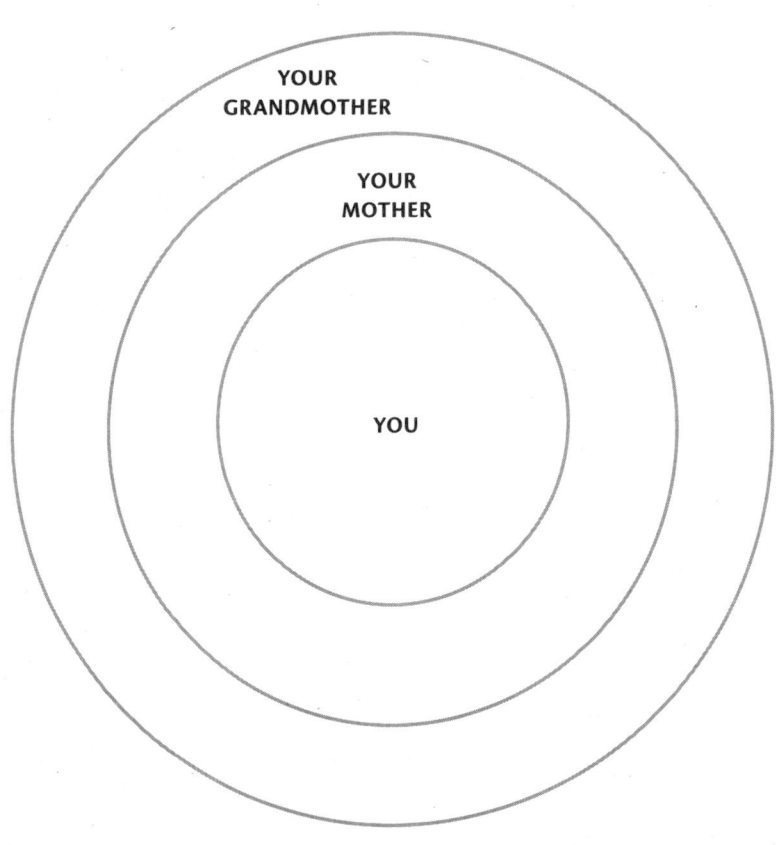

What patterns do you notice?

....
....
....

Which generation may have experienced a break in the mother-child bond? What happened?

....
....
....

Which one of you may have experienced the most severe attachment trauma?

....

Did trauma in one generation affect behaviors in the next? If so, please explain.

....
....
....

Could you be experiencing your grandmother's or mother's trauma response? If so, say more.

....

....

....

WHY ATTACHMENT TRAUMA IS EASY TO MISS

When we've experienced a break in the bond with our mother, the effects can be devastating. And yet they're easy to miss.

The trauma often happens before we're able to form memories. Perhaps you've grown up in a warm and loving home with attentive parents, and yet you struggle with unexplained symptoms such as anxiety, depression, difficulties in relationships, or a feeling that something just isn't right. Why would you believe you've experienced trauma if you have no memory of it?

Because we don't remember our experiences until somewhere around age three, we don't have clear memories of our mother's care when we were in utero and during the first couple years of life, when the brain is being wired for safety or hypervigilance. For example, if we were in an incubator during that period, or our mother gave us to our grandmother to raise for a month because she was stressed or working, or our father and mother split up, or our mother had postpartum depression, or if there were a miscarriage before us, we simply wouldn't know unless we asked.

The trauma tends to be cumulative. Attachment trauma generally doesn't result from just one or two short lapses in care. We're designed to be resilient and can bounce back from that. It's unrealistic to expect a mother to be perfectly attuned to her child 100 percent of the time. Psychologists Donald Winnicott and Edward Tronick tell us that a mother's attunement only needs to be in sync with her infant's emotional needs about 30 percent of the time for her child to feel secure.[5] Disruptions are bound to happen. When they do, the repair process can be a positive growth experience, giving both mother and child an opportunity to learn how to handle brief moments of distress and then reach out for each other to reconnect again. What is most important is that the repair is made. Repeatedly repairing a relationship actually builds a sense of trust and resilience and helps to create a secure attachment between mother and child.[6]

Yet, when there are too many or continual lapses in care that never get repaired, it can break the attachment. Maybe our mother was unhappy in her relationship. Maybe she felt trapped by the pregnancy and was forced to marry. Maybe she felt that being a mom caused her to shelve her dreams. All these experiences, and more, could have eroded her attunement, often with no fault of her own. Because there's no magic number for "too many" lapses or "too long" of a break in attunement, it can be hard to define.

The trauma can occur anytime throughout our first decade of life. Although it's true that our brain develops like wildfire in the womb and through the first few years of life, it continues to develop dramatically through our first decade and beyond. If we experience too many physical or emotional separations from our mother during our first ten or so years, it can create a break in the bond.

Here are some examples:

- ▶ Your mom was institutionalized for a few weeks when you were seven.
- ▶ You were in the hospital with a serious condition for a month when you were eight.
- ▶ Your parents were divorced at age five, and from then on you spent half your time with your dad and half with your mom.
- ▶ Starting at age three, you spent every summer with your grandparents.

We can inherit our parents' attachment trauma through the sperm cell or egg cell. As we discussed above, even if we had a "good enough" relationship with our mother, we can still inherit her or our father's fight, flight, freeze responses from their break in the attachment with their mother. And it will be a mystery to us why we feel the way we feel. If our mother or father, for example, experienced a severe separation such as losing their mother, being given away to relatives or to another family, or being placed in foster care, we can inherit their feelings and sensations and never make the link that we're sharing the family nervous system.

In light of this, you may be wondering why we don't all have attachment trauma! The truth is that many of us do and just don't realize it. The good news is that humans are designed to be resilient, and the majority of us who have experienced a break in the bond with our mother still got enough of what we needed—even with the deficits.

There are no hard-and-fast rules as to what behavior causes trauma and what does not. Often trauma only reveals itself through its effects—which is why exploring our own uncomfortable experiences and history is so important. Even when our connection to our mother is relatively intact, we may still find ourselves grappling with feelings we don't understand. We might struggle with fears of being left, rejected, or abandoned, or feelings of being exposed, humiliated, or shamed, or beliefs that we're not enough, or we're too much, or we don't matter, or we're not important.

However, when these feelings are understood in the context of our early relationship with our mother—likely from a time we don't remember—we can become more aware of what was missing and what we need in order to heal.

# EXERCISE
WHAT I BELIEVE ABOUT MYSELF

If you're wondering whether or not you've experienced an attachment trauma, let's explore some of the feelings, emotions, thoughts, and beliefs you may have about yourself.

Are there situations in which you feel that you're not good enough? Situations in which you feel invisible or discounted or ignored? Maybe you don't feel seen, or heard, or understood. Maybe you feel that you don't matter. Or you're not important. Or you're not enough, but if you express yourself, you'll be too much. Maybe you feel there's something wrong with you, and you'll be judged, humiliated, rejected, or left. Maybe you fear you'll be all alone, and no one will love you.

Do you recognize any of these thoughts, feelings, or beliefs? If so, write them down here.

....

....

....

# EXERCISE

HOW I EXPERIENCE MYSELF IN RELATIONSHIPS

As I said earlier, what's unresolved in our early relationship with our mother is often projected onto our partners, and we will feel with them the way we felt with her.

Think about your current romantic relationship. If you're not in a relationship now, imagine your most recent relationship.

In this relationship, do/did you trust easily? Do you feel supported? Do you feel considered? Do you feel heard? Or do you feel unseen, that you're not a priority, that you don't matter, that you're not important? Describe your experience.

....

....

....

....

....

How do you experience your partner's behaviors toward you?

....

....

....

EXERCISE
WHAT HAPPENED?

In the next chapter, we'll delve more deeply into the break in the bond. But at this point, I'd like to check in with you. What do you think happened in your early relationship with your mother, or in your family history, that may have disrupted the bond between you and your mother?

....
....
....
....
....

If nothing came to you, consider these questions:

What do you know about your mother's pregnancy with you?

- ▶ Was she happy with your father?
- ▶ Was he happy with her?
- ▶ Did she want to have a child?
- ▶ Did she lose a child or a pregnancy before you?
- ▶ Were they married when you were conceived?

- Was anybody drinking, or cheating, or trying to leave the relationship?
- Did the pregnancy go smoothly?

....
....
....

What do you know about your first few years of life?

- Did something happen to you or to your mother that separated you either physically or emotionally?
- Was your mother overwhelmed or deeply stressed?
- Did she have postpartum depression?
- Were you hospitalized during this period? Was she?
- Did you spend days, weeks, months, or even years away from your mother?
- Did your parents stay together?

....
....
....

How did your childhood go?

- ▶ Did your parents get along, or was your home chaotic?
- ▶ Was your mom's attention pulled away from you?
- ▶ Did you have a sibling that required her constant attention?
- ▶ Did your mom travel, take an extended vacation, or have to be away from home for a long period of time?

....
....
....

To answer these questions fully, you may want to let a day or two go by to allow more thoughts and memories to rise to the surface.

We may think that the more vivid and emotional a memory is, the more traumatic it is, but in the case of attachment trauma, the opposite may be true. If one or more of the above experiences happened to you, even if you have no memory of it and no emotional reaction to it, it still could have affected your nervous system and disrupted your sense of well-being. Ultimately, if you didn't feel seen, known, or soothed in your relationship with your mother—that's an attachment trauma.

Even if you didn't experience a trauma with your mother, as I mentioned above, you could still have inherited the fragments of gene expression from a break in the bond that happened with your parents or grandparents and their mothers.

- ▶ Do you recall any family stories about something distressing or traumatic that happened to your parents or grandparents when they were small that may have affected their relationship with their mothers? Did your mother or father, or any of your grandparents, spend time away from their mothers when they were young?
- ▶ Were they adopted?
- ▶ Did they spend time in foster care?
- ▶ Did your grandmother or great-grandmother die in childbirth?
- ▶ Did a parent or grandparent feel emotionally disconnected from their mother?

....
....
....
....
....

Now look at what you've written. Do you believe you had a break in the bond with your mother, or a break in the bond in the family that traveled downstream to you? Before we go further, I recommend taking a day or two to mull this over. Then, when you're ready, come back and we'll deepen the journey by diving into the Four Unconscious Themes.

CHAPTER 3

THE FOUR UNCONSCIOUS THEMES

Now let's take a look at how our ability to flourish in life can be constrained by unconscious family relationships. I've discovered that there are four themes operating beneath the surface that can cause suffering:

1. We have merged with a parent.
2. We have rejected a parent.
3. We have experienced a break in the bond with our mother.
4. We have identified with a member of our family system other than our parents.

These four unconscious themes represent four ways life's forward progress can be hindered—four ways success, health, vitality, and relationships can be diminished. I use these themes as tools to determine how to help my clients.

You can use these themes the same way. Let's begin.

1.

HAVE YOU MERGED WITH A PARENT?

When we've merged with a parent, we share or repeat an aspect of that parent's life experience, often a negative experience—a way they suffered, a misfortune they endured—and we do so as an unconscious way of bonding with them.

For example, our parent is in poor health or is morbidly obese, and we share compromised health with this parent by smoking, drinking excessively, overeating, or refusing to make time for exercise. Or our parent is mistreated by the other parent, and we allow ourselves to be mistreated by our partner, or we mistreat our partner in a similar way. Or our parent gave away a child, or lost custody, and we either abort or sever our connection with our child.

Four Ways of Merging

- ▶ **I'll follow you.** In this dynamic, a child might try to die early to join his or her deceased parent in death by taking drugs, driving recklessly, practicing extreme sports, or engaging in other high-risk behaviors.

- **I'll share it with you.** In this dynamic, a child might try to join a parent in his or her misfortune: the parent may have been treated poorly in his or her relationship, lost their great love, drank too much, failed financially, lived in poor health, et cetera, and the child repeats the behavior.

- **I'll do it in your place.** In this dynamic, a child might take on emotions the parent couldn't process: "If you can't feel the grief of what happened to you, I'll feel all of it." Or, "If you're unhappy and want to die, I'll become depressed, anorexic, or suicidal."

- **I'll atone for you.** In this dynamic, a child unconsciously pays for something that happened in the past: "I'll go to jail, or take my life, or become sick to atone for what you did."

EXERCISE

HAVE I MERGED WITH MY PARENT?

Do you suspect that you've merged with the feelings, or behaviors, or experience of a parent? Consider the following questions. Don't limit yourself to a yes or no; write down your full thoughts and feelings about what you experienced.

Did one of your parents struggle physically or emotionally? How so?

....
....
....

Do you experience a similar struggle in your life? If so, say more.

....
....
....

Did it hurt you to see them suffer? Did you want to take their pain away? Did you try? If so, what did that look like?

....
....
....

Did you side with the feelings of one parent against the other? If so, how?

....
....
....

Were you afraid to show your love to one parent for fear of hurting the other? How so?

....

....

....

How do you experience your parents' pain in your life?

....

....

....

2.

HAVE YOU REJECTED A PARENT?

Our life—our very existence—comes to us from our parents. That life force, however, the vitality that animates our being, can become blocked when we've rejected, judged, blamed, or distanced ourselves from one or both of our parents. We might not be consciously aware of it, but pushing a parent away is akin to pushing away a part of ourselves.

Let's see if that's true for you. Tune in to the energetic connection you have with your parents, the way you allow them into your heart or block them from entering.

 **PRACTICE**
Sensing the Flow

Take a minute and feel the connection or disconnection you have with your parents. Regardless of the story you have about them, feel the relationship and how it affects your body physically.

Visualize your biological parents standing in front of you. If you have never met them or cannot visualize them, just let yourself sense their presence. Hold the image and ask yourself the following:

- Do I welcome them, or do I shut them out?
- Do I sense them as welcoming me?
- Do I experience one differently from the other?
- Is my body relaxed or tight as I visualize them?
- If a life-giving force were flowing from them to me, how much of it would be getting through?

    5 percent?

    25 percent?

    50 percent?

    75 percent?

Or a full 100 percent?

How Much I Let Myself Receive from My Mother:

....

How Much I Let Myself Receive from My Father:

....

When we reject a parent—either parent—there are three ways that rejection can operate unconsciously inside us:

- ▶ **We reject a part of ourselves.** The behaviors we dislike in our parents, the behaviors we view as negative in them, get disowned in us, and then can express unconsciously. Blind to how their behaviors also live in us, we can't see when we're the same. When we behave coldly or meanly, or when we become distant or aggressive, we rarely make the link that we're sharing this behavior with them.

- ▶ **Our unhealed relationship with our parent gets projected onto others.** We'll either pull in partners with similar traits who treat us in the same way as our parents, or we'll do the opposite; we'll attract caring partners, yet see them as uncaring. We'll interpret their actions in the most negative light. In our hypervigilance and inability to trust, we could even turn a good partner into a bad one.

▶ **We'll do to ourselves the very thing we believe was done to us.** If our parent was critical or aggressive, we can become self-critical and inwardly aggressive, treating our inner child in the same way. Or if our parent ignored us, we can ignore that young, vulnerable part of ourselves.

In recognizing these dynamics, we need to ask ourselves: Have we judged, blamed, rejected, or distanced ourselves from either parent? Could we go to one for comfort, but not the other?

It's important to ask these questions. As you'll learn later, the very language we use to describe our parents ("Mother is selfish, cruel, and vindictive") can mirror the relationships we have with our partner, our friends, our boss, our coworkers, and even with ourselves.

 **EXERCISE**

HAVE I REJECTED A PARENT?

Consider the following questions. Again, these are not yes-or-no answers. Please write down whatever thoughts, feelings, or memories come to mind.

Do you reject, blame, or judge a parent for something you feel he or she has done to you?

....

....

Could you go to one parent for comfort, but not the other?

....

Do you treat one or both of your parents disrespectfully?

....

Have you cut yourself off from either of them?

....

Consider the three ways a rejection of your parent may operate unconsciously in you.

How do you see the behaviors you experience in your parents living in you? How do you act similarly?

PARENT'S BEHAVIORS	HOW I BEHAVE SIMILARLY

Describe your current or most recent intimate relationship. How are/were you treated? How do/did you treat this partner? Do you see any similarities in the way your parent(s) treated you?

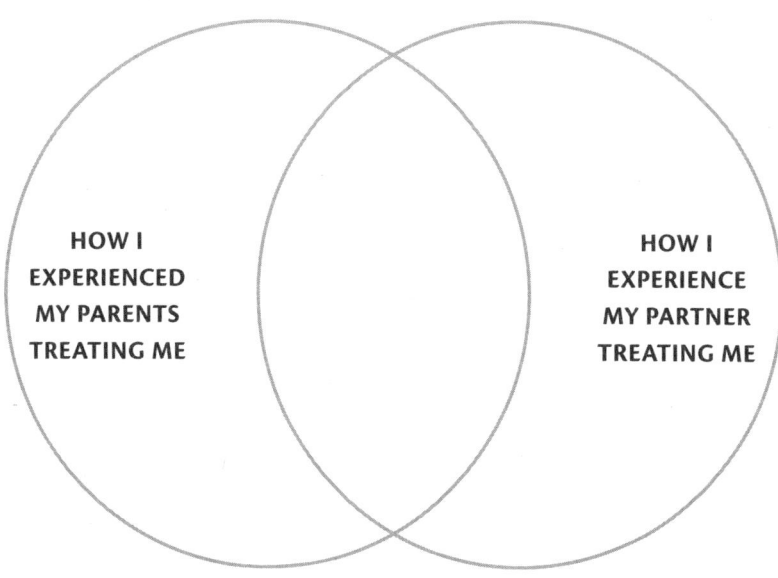

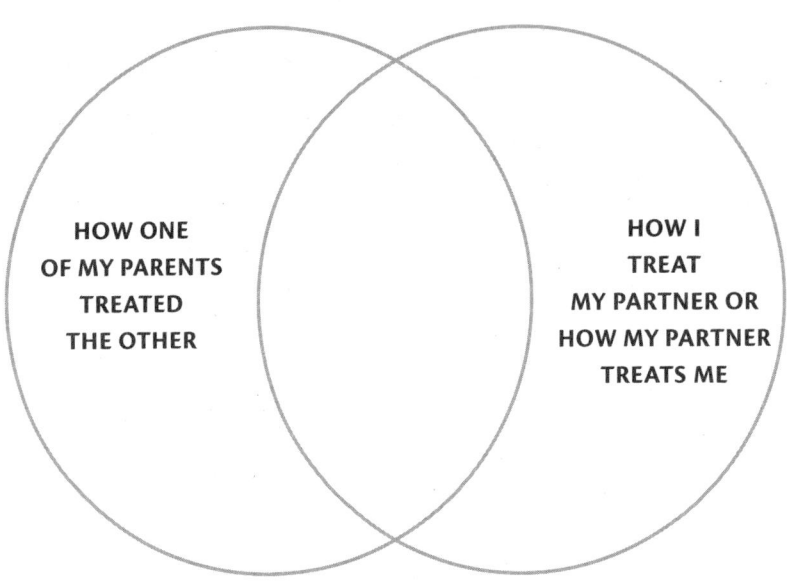

How might you treat yourself the same way you believe your parent(s) treated you? For example, if you felt ignored, do you ignore that young, vulnerable part of yourself?

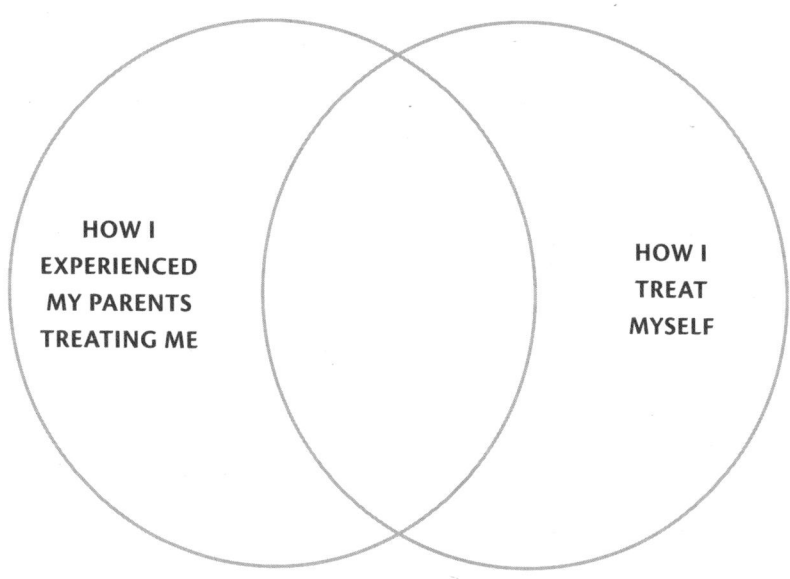

3.

DID YOU EXPERIENCE A BREAK IN THE BOND WITH YOUR MOTHER?

If you reject your mother, it could be that you also experienced an interruption during the early bonding process with her. Yet not everyone who experiences a break in the early bond will reject their mother. What is more likely is that you experience some degree of anxiety when you attempt to bond with a partner in an intimate relationship. That anxiety could translate into difficulty trusting your partner, difficulty calming yourself when you feel triggered, difficulty staying in a relationship, or perhaps not even wanting a relationship at all. It could also translate into making the decision not to have children. On the surface, you might complain that raising a child involves too much time and energy. On the deeper level, you might feel ill-equipped to supply a child with what you yourself have missed.

 EXERCISE

HAVE I EXPERIENCED A BREAK IN THE BOND WITH MY MOTHER?

Since a break in the bond often occurs before we form memories, how do we know if we've experienced one?

You've already done the hard part. Revisit your answers to the exercise "What Happened?" in chapter 2. Now I'm going to ask you these questions again. If you're not sure about the answers, ask your mother. If she's not alive or if she's unwilling to discuss it with you, ask another family member—an aunt, uncle, cousin, friend of the family—someone who may know what happened. Feeling guilt or shame, our mothers might not always share events that were uncomfortable.

> ▶ *Did something traumatic happen while your mother was pregnant with you? Was she highly anxious, depressed, or stressed?*

....

> ▶ *Were your parents having difficulties in their relationship during the pregnancy or in your early childhood? (Unsure they'd stay together? Violence? Arguing? Separating? Drinking? Cheating?) Did your mother give away a child or lose a child or pregnancy before you were born?*

....

> ▶ *Did you experience a difficult birth? (Did your mother have a protracted labor? Were you born premature or by C-section? Were forceps used? Did either you or your mother experience medical distress?)*

....

▶ Did your mother experience a complication from the pregnancy and have to be hospitalized?

....

▶ Did you spend time in an incubator or the neonatal ICU?

....

▶ Were you separated from your mother after birth?

....

▶ Were you adopted?

....

▶ Did your mother experience postpartum depression?

....

▶ Did you experience a trauma or a separation from your mother during your childhood or infancy? (Were either you or your mother ever hospitalized and forced to be apart? Did your parents leave you to go on a vacation? Were you sent to stay with grandparents or other family members?)

....

▶ *Did your mother experience a trauma or emotional turmoil during your childhood or infancy (the death of a parent, grandparent, sibling, or child, a separation or divorce, etc.)?*

....

▶ *Was your mother's attention pulled to a trauma involving one of your siblings when you were young (a late-term miscarriage, a stillbirth, a death, a medical emergency, etc.)?*

....

▶ *Did any other trauma happen to your mother that affected her ability to be attentive? Was she present with you? Or preoccupied?*

....

▶ *Did your mother seem disconnected when she touched you? In the way she looked at you? In the tone of her voice when she spoke to you?*

....

▶ *Do you experience difficulty bonding in a relationship? Do you shut down, pull away, or push away from closeness?*

....

After reading through these questions, what did you or your mother experience that may have created a break in the attachment?

....
....
....
....
....

4.

DID YOU UNCONSCIOUSLY IDENTIFY WITH A MEMBER OF YOUR FAMILY SYSTEM OTHER THAN YOUR PARENTS?

Sometimes, our relationship with our parents is strong and loving, yet we still find ourselves unable to explain the difficult feelings we carry. We often assume that the problem originates inside us, and if we only dig deep enough, we'll discover its source. Until we uncover the actual triggering event in our family history, we can relive fears and feelings that don't belong to us—unconscious fragments of a trauma—and think they're ours.

The renowned German psychotherapist Bert Hellinger called this mechanism *unconscious loyalty* and viewed this as the cause of much suffering in families. He taught that everyone has the same right to belong in a family system, and that no one can be excluded for any reason whatsoever. This includes the alcoholic grandfather who left our grandmother impoverished, the stillborn brother whose death broke our mother's heart, and even the neighbor's child our father accidently killed as he backed out of the driveway. The criminal uncle, our mother's older half sister, the baby we aborted—they all belong in our family. The list goes on.

Even people we wouldn't normally consider part of our family system must be included. If someone harmed or murdered or took advantage of a member of our family, that person must be included. Likewise, if somebody in our family harmed or murdered or took advantage of someone, that victim would also need to be included in our family system.

Earlier partners of our parents and grandparents also belong. By their dying or leaving or having been left, an opening is created that allows for our mother, father, grandmother, or grandfather to enter the system, and ultimately allows for us to be born.

Hellinger observed that when someone is rejected or left out of the family system, that person can be represented by a later member of the system. The later person might share or repeat the earlier person's fate by behaving similarly or by repeating some aspect of the excluded person's suffering. If, for example, your grandfather is rejected in the family because of his drinking, gambling, and philandering, it is possible that one or more of these behaviors will be adopted by one of his descendants. In this way, family suffering continues into subsequent generations.

When we have an identification with a forgotten, or hated, or rejected, or pitied member of our family, we can live like, feel like, or behave like them by reenacting aspects of their traumatic experience. We're most likely to take on the traits of a family member when that person isn't spoken about. This can be a victim, a perpetrator, a criminal, a murderer, an alcoholic, a loner, someone who suffered deeply, someone of the opposite sex, someone who was wronged or who wronged others, someone who died early, someone who grieved a great loss, and more.

EXERCISE

AM I UNCONSCIOUSLY IDENTIFIED WITH A MEMBER OF MY FAMILY SYSTEM OTHER THAN MY PARENTS?

Could you be feeling like, behaving like, suffering like, atoning for, or carrying the grief of someone who came before you? Consider the following questions. Write down any thoughts, feelings, or stories you remember about any rejected, ignored, hated, or pitied person who came before you, such as the family black sheep or villain.

Do you have symptoms, feelings, or behaviors that are difficult to explain in the context of your life experience?

....

....

....

Did someone do something that caused his or her rejection in your family?

....
....
....

Did guilt or pain prevent a family member from loving or grieving fully?

....
....
....

Was there a trauma in the family (an early death of a parent, child, or sibling, or an abandonment, murder, crime, or suicide)— an event that was too terrible, painful, or shameful to talk about?

....
....
....

Could you be connected with that event, living a life similar to the person no one talks about? Or connected to the person who experienced that pain, loss, or suffering?

....

Could you be reliving this family member's trauma as though it were your own?

THOUGHTS, FEELINGS, EMOTIONS, SYMPTOMS, AND BEHAVIORS THAT SEEM OUT OF CONTEXT IN MY LIFE	PERSON(S) I MAY BE IDENTIFIED WITH	WHAT HAPPENED TO THEM

THE SIBLING CONNECTION

If you have siblings, just because you share the same family doesn't mean you carry the same trauma. Even children born of the same parents, in the same family home, who share a similar upbringing, are likely to inherit different traumas and experience different fates. For example, the firstborn son is likely to carry what remains unresolved with the father, and the firstborn daughter is likely to carry what remains unresolved with the mother, though this is not always the case. The reverse can also be true. Later children in the family are likely to carry different aspects of their parents' traumas, or elements of the grandparents' traumas.

For example, the first daughter might marry a man who is emotionally unavailable and controlling—similar to how she perceives her father—and, by doing so, share this dynamic with her mother. By marrying a shut-down, controlling man, she repeats her mother's experiences and joins her in her discontent. The second daughter might carry the unexpressed anger of her mother. In this way, she is affected by the same trauma, but expresses a different aspect of it. She might even reject her father, whereas the first daughter does not. In the same family, either the third or fourth daughter might never marry, fearing that she will be controlled by a man she doesn't love.

I once worked with a Lebanese family that shared a similar dynamic. When we looked back another generation, we learned that both of the Lebanese grandmothers were given away by their parents to become child brides—the one grandmother at age nine and the other at age twelve. Connected with their grandmothers' experience of being forced to marry while still children, two of the Lebanese sisters repeated aspects of this fate in their relationships. Like her grandmothers, one married a much older man. The other never married at all, complaining that men were disgusting—similar to how her unhappy paternal grandmother must have felt being trapped in a loveless marriage.

If multiple siblings experience a break in the mother-child bond, each child might express his or her disconnection with the mother differently. One child might become a people pleaser, fearing that if he's not good, or he makes waves, he'll lose connection with people. Another child, believing that connection is never hers to have in the first place, might become argumentative and create conflict to push away the people close to her. Another child might isolate and have little contact with people at all.

I've noticed that if several siblings have breaks in the mother-child bond, they'll often express anger or jealousy, or feel disconnected from one another. For example, an older child might resent the child born later, perceiving that the younger child received the love he or she did not get. Because the hippocampus—that part of the brain involved in creating memories—isn't fully operational until after the age of two, the older child may not consciously remember being held, fed, or cuddled by the mother, but remembers the younger child receiving their mother's love. In response, the older child, feeling slighted, can unconsciously blame the younger child for getting what he or she did not.

And then, of course, there are some children who don't seem to carry any family trauma at all. For these children, it's quite possible that a successful bond was established with the mother and/or father, and this connection helped to immunize the child from carrying entanglements from the past. Perhaps a window of time opened in which the mother was able to give more to one particular child and not the others. Perhaps the parents' relationship improved. Perhaps the mother experienced a special connection with one child, but couldn't connect deeply with the others. Younger children often, though not always, seem to do a bit better than first children or only children, who tend to carry a bigger portion of unfinished business from the family history.

When it comes to siblings and inherited family trauma, there are no hard and fast rules governing how each child is affected. Many variables, in addition to birth order and gender, can influence the choices siblings make and the lives they lead. Even though it may appear from the outside that one sibling is unscathed by trauma while another is encumbered, my clinical experience gives me a different perspective: Most of us carry at least some residue from our family history.

Do you have a sibling? If so, how do you and your siblings lead different lives?

Here are some questions to consider:

- *Did you have a sibling who didn't leave the family home or succeed in life?*
- *Was one the peacemaker in the family?*
- *Did one function as a caretaker for your parents?*
- *Did one reject your parents?*
- *Was one the black sheep?*
- *Did one struggle with chronic illness or failed relationships?*
- *Did one sibling seem to have it all?*

....
....
....
....
....

 **EXERCISE**

WHICH OF THE FOUR UNCONSCIOUS THEMES IS PART OF YOUR STORY?

Now that you've had time to sit with each of the themes, do you recognize one or more of them in yourself? Consider the following questions:

Which theme are you most aware of in your life? How might it be limiting you?

....

....

....

Which theme piqued your interest most when you read about it?

....

....

....

Do you connect with more than one theme? Which one(s)?

....

....

....

In the chart below, describe how you are experiencing the theme(s) playing out in your life.

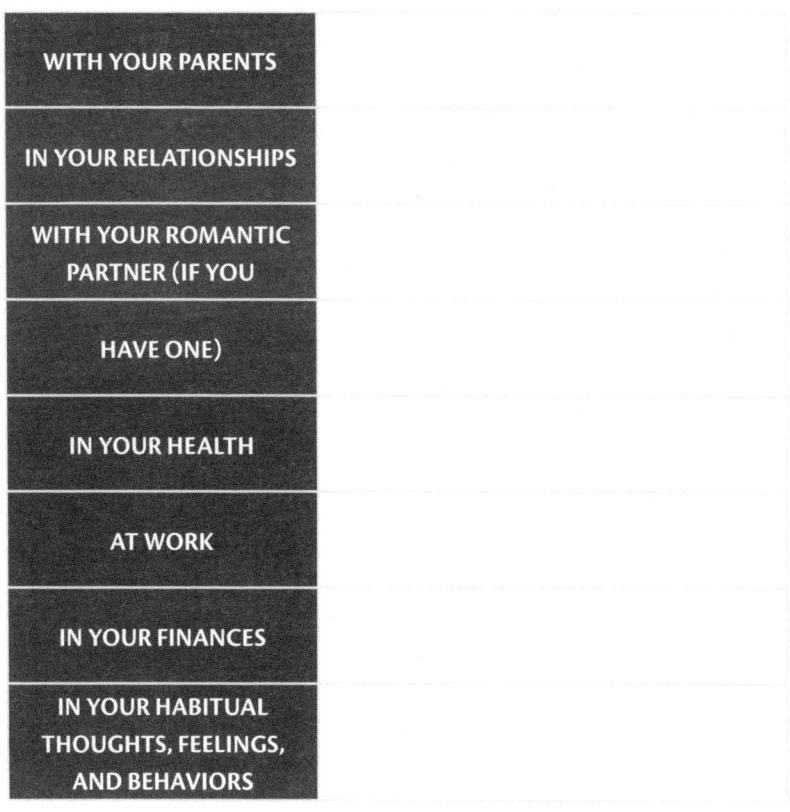

WITH YOUR PARENTS	
IN YOUR RELATIONSHIPS	
WITH YOUR ROMANTIC PARTNER (IF YOU HAVE ONE)	
IN YOUR HEALTH	
AT WORK	
IN YOUR FINANCES	
IN YOUR HABITUAL THOUGHTS, FEELINGS, AND BEHAVIORS	

As you think about these themes, you may find that more than one applies to you. Did you reject one parent and merge with the other? Did something break the bond with your mother? Many of us have more than one theme operating in the background. In later chapters, we'll address each theme in detail.

Susan contacted me because she wanted to work on her relationship with her partner of twenty-seven years. They cared deeply about each other, but Susan felt she always kept him at arm's length and had difficulty receiving his love. Even though she had a fully committed partner and a solid support system, she felt alone and somehow responsible for everyone and everything. For as long as she could remember, she felt the effects of trauma in her life and yet couldn't identify any trauma in her history.

Seemingly unrelated, Susan had begun to develop physical symptoms on her left side: her left shoulder had become too painful to move, and she'd lost dexterity in her left hand. The many doctors she had consulted offered a variety of explanations—a pinched nerve, a frozen shoulder, perimenopause—yet she wondered if these symptoms had a deeper meaning.

"Tell me about your mother's pregnancy with you," I asked. "What do you imagine your mom was feeling or thinking when you were in her womb? Was she happy with your father back then? Did she want to have a child with him, or was she feeling trapped?"

"She and my dad had a good relationship, and she was excited to be pregnant," Susan answered, "but she may have been worried she'd lose me. My mom had four miscarriages, but I'm not sure when they were."

When miscarriages happen, it's important to know when they occur and whether they're early- or late-term. As we learned earlier, when a pregnant mother experiences significant stress or trauma, her stress hormones flood into the amniotic fluid, and this can affect the crucial neural development of her baby. If Susan's mother lost a baby previously, she would have likely been terrified she'd lose Susan as well. *Don't attach to the baby before it's born, because the baby could die.* And if that miscarriage occurred late-term, the loss of that pregnancy could feel even more traumatic.

"Is your mom available now?" I asked. "Could you call her and ask when the miscarriages happened, and if they were early-term or late-term?"

Fortunately, Susan was willing to call her mother, and her mother answered. She discovered that not only did her mother have two late-term miscarriages before Susan was born, she had a third late-term miscarriage when Susan was two. This meant Susan lost her mother twice: once in the womb, as her mother was preparing herself for the potential loss of another baby, and once to the grief her mother felt when she actually lost another baby, during a time that was crucial for Susan's neurodevelopment. Susan had experienced two massive attachment traumas, of which she knew nothing—until she asked her mother for this critical information.

Susan's primary unconscious theme: a break in the bond

Jordan, a forty-two-year-old systems analyst, wanted to understand the severe anxiety and panic disorder he had struggled with since he was seventeen. Along with the visceral feelings of his heart beating out of his chest, tight lungs, and a terror of blacking out, he carried an obsessive fear of harming someone close to him.

"When you're anxious like this," I asked him, "what goes through your head?"

"That I'll do something terrible. I'll harm someone I care about, and it will all be my fault."

"Have you ever done something to harm someone?" I asked.

"No, never."

If this worry didn't come from Jordan's experience, I wondered who the family member was that Jordan had merged or identified with.

"Did something happen to a parent or another family member when they were seventeen?"

"I'm not sure."

"Do you know if anyone in your family harmed someone?"

"Not that I know of."

Even if Jordan didn't know this information, it was important for him to find out. I asked him to call his parents, who fortunately were both still alive, and ask. In the chapters that follow, you'll see how his exploration led him to the answer he needed.

Jordan's primary unconscious theme: merging with a parent, or an identification with another family member

So far, you've learned about the potential effects of inherited and attachment trauma, you've had an opportunity to think about your own family stories, and you've explored how you might be entangled with one or both of your parents, or with another family member.

Now it's time to apply what you've learned.

To unearth the traumas buried in your life experiences and in your very words, you'll construct your own *core language map*, beginning with the next chapter. This map will lead you through a healing journey, and home to yourself.

INTRODUCTION TO THE CORE LANGUAGE APPROACH

The unspoken experiences that live in our unconscious, reflected in the four unconscious themes, are all around us. They appear in our quirky language. They express in our chronic symptoms and unexplainable behaviors. They resurface in the repetitive struggles we face in our day-to-day lives. These unspoken experiences form the basis of our *core language*. When our unconscious breaks down our door to be heard, core language is what we hear.

The emotionally charged words and sentences of our core language likely stem from unresolved trauma and are the keys to unearthing memories that live both in our body and in the "body" of our family system. They are like gems in our unconscious waiting to be excavated. If we fail to recognize them as messengers, we miss important clues that can help us unravel the mystery behind our struggles. Once we dig them out, we take an essential step toward healing.

Simply put, core language helps us piece together the events and experiences at the root of our suffering. When enough of these pieces are gathered in our consciousness, we begin to form a story that deepens our understanding of what might have happened to us or to our family members. We begin to make sense of the memories, emotions, and sensations that may have been haunting us our entire lives. Once we locate their origin in the past, in our trauma or in a family trauma, we can stop living them as though they belong in the present. And though not every fear, anxiety, or repetitive thought can be explained by a traumatic event in the family, certain experiences can be more fully understood when we decipher the language in our core complaint, core descriptors, and core sentence—which you're about to discover for yourself.

Types of Core Language

Core language can be split into two types: verbal and nonverbal. When it's verbal, it lives in the intense or urgent words we use to describe our deepest fears and anxieties. We can also hear it in the complaints we have about our relationships, our health, our work, and other life situations. This trauma language is unusual in that it can feel out of context from what we know or what we have experienced. Verbal core language can have the quality of coming from outside us while being experienced inside us.

When it's nonverbal, we find it in our behaviors and symptoms. It lives in our depression, in the destructive behaviors that mimic certain traumatic events in our family history, in the unusual symptoms that show up after an unsettling situation, in the fears and anxieties that strike suddenly when we reach a certain age—often the same age that something traumatic happened in a past generation. Nonverbal core language is also mirrored in our relationship struggles, the types of partners we choose, how we allow ourselves to be treated, and how we treat others, as well as in the repeated ways we deal with money and success. Nonverbal core language is even revealed in the way we've disconnected from our bodies, and from the core of ourselves. Essentially, it's the fallout from trauma that has occurred in our early childhood or family history. All of this forms a breadcrumb trail that can lead us quickly to the source of our issue.

Your Core Language Map

There are four steps to constructing your core language map. In each step, you will be given a new tool. Each tool is designed to extract new information. The tools are:

1. The Core Complaint
2. The Core Descriptors
3. The Core Sentence
4. The Core Trauma

Following your core language map can bring you face-to-face with family members who live like ghosts, unseen and ignored. Some have been long buried. Some have been rejected or forgotten. Others have gone through ordeals so traumatic, it's too painful to think about what they must have endured. Once you find them, they are set free and you are set free.

Your history is waiting to be discovered. The words, the language, the map—everything you need to make the journey is inside you at this very moment. And it all starts with what brought you to this work in the first place: your *core complaint*.

CHAPTER 4

YOUR CORE COMPLAINT

As you construct your core language map, you will learn to follow your words as they form a trail of clues that lead you to the origin of your fears. Along this verbal path, the core complaint will be your first stopping point. It can be a treasure chest of unexamined wealth. It can even contain the seeds of the resolution you seek. You just need to look inside.

To hear the core complaint in our everyday language, we look for the deepest thread of emotion in the fabric of the words we speak. We listen for words that have the strongest emotional resonance to them. Sometimes there is a debilitating fear that holds us captive. Sometimes there's an urgent quality to something being asked for or requested.

Sometimes there's just great pain. Sometimes we hear words or phrases that appear to have a life of their own.

In analyzing the core complaint, we not only listen to our spoken language, we observe our somatic or physical body language as well. We also pay particularly close attention to the symptoms and behaviors we have that stand out as idiosyncratic or unusual.

When we examine the words of a core complaint, we trust the words implicitly. We don't always trust the context, however. The words themselves are generally true for someone—not necessarily us. Discovering who that someone is requires a peek behind the curtain into our family history.

DISCOVERING YOUR CORE COMPLAINT

Let's begin our excavation by examining the issue that brought you here in the first place. What feels most pressing in your life right now? Does it relate to your health? Your job? Your relationship? It can be any issue that disrupts your sense of safety, peace, security, or well-being.

What do you want to heal? What do you want to see shift?

....

....

....

....

....

Don't edit yourself. Write down whatever feels important to you. Write it down as it comes to you. You may carry a fear of something terrible happening to you in the future. You may have a problem that feels overwhelming to you. It may be feelings of discontent you have toward someone close to you. It may be a symptom or feeling you've had all your life. It doesn't matter what comes out; just keep writing.

If nothing comes, answer this one question: If the feeling or symptom or condition you have never goes away, what would you be afraid could happen to you?

....

....

....

Don't continue reading until you've written down your most pressing concern.

Now look at what you've written. As you read it, don't read it so carefully that you become enthralled with it. Don't get caught up in the words or feelings. Scan it lightly without feeling the emotions. You're looking for words or phrases that stand out as unusual or peculiar. For example, what words or phrases do you always say, or perhaps have never said before this writing exercise? What language seems to jump out at you? What language calls out to be noticed?

Words or phrases that stand out to you:

....

....

....

Now read your response again. But this time, read it out loud to yourself. Try to hear with a new ear, without feeling emotions. I call this type of listening "hearing with our meta ear" or "hearing with our third ear." What words or sentences have an urgent quality to them? What words have a strong emotional resonance or a dramatic feeling? What words have a feeling of strangeness or peculiarity? What words may not fit entirely in the context of your life experience?

Words or phrases that sound dramatic, urgent, or strange:

....

....

....

See if you can listen to what you've written as though you were listening to someone else. Perhaps the words do in fact belong to someone else, and you have merely been giving them a voice. Perhaps the words belong to someone in your family who was traumatized and couldn't speak them out loud. Maybe through your complaints, you are telling this person's story.

> **In our initial conversation,** Jordan named his core complaint easily: he had experienced constant anxiety since age seventeen, as well as a persistent feeling that he would harm someone close to him. When Jordan told me he hadn't personally hurt anyone, I sensed there was more to the story. Since this type of language—harming another—is more likely to stem from someone older rather than from someone younger, I surmised the story likely belonged to an adult—but who? Hold that piece of the puzzle; we'll find out in a later chapter.
>
> **Jordan's core complaint:** constant anxiety, and a persistent feeling he would harm someone close to him

If your core complaint seems to have nothing to do with your family history, I recommend you reread the section on the break in the bond in chapter 2. Perhaps these words are your words—from a trauma you experienced in the womb, or in your early childhood—long before your memory could claim them as your own.

> **Susan's core complaint** was about her relationship: "I know my husband loves me, and I love him, but I feel like my heart is behind glass. I just don't feel connected. Even though he's always there for me, I feel overwhelmed most of the time, like I have to take care of everyone and everything. I don't trust anyone to take care of me."

Can you hear how an infant who experienced a break in the bond might feel the same way: "overwhelmed," not "connected," and unable to "trust anyone to take care" of her?

Susan had also shared with me that she had a frozen shoulder that kept her from completing even simple tasks without pain. Yet she soldiered on. We talked about the metaphor of a frozen shoulder, how she was shouldering the burden of taking care of everyone and everything on her own.

She told me that, in her childhood, she could never go to her mother for comfort when she was scared or upset, and ultimately had to comfort herself. But how can a child with feelings she doesn't understand soothe herself? She can't. Those feelings often submerge, only to reappear later in life in the form of symptoms—especially when we feel triggered in our relationships.

Susan's core complaint: distance in her relationship, and a frozen shoulder

Sometimes, like Susan's, our core complaint shows up in nonverbal ways—symptoms or issues that speak louder than words. Maybe you have a physical symptom, a chronic or autoimmune condition, or experience repeated injuries. Maybe you have a diagnosis like depression, lupus, or cancer. Maybe you have symptoms that have mystified doctors and professionals, and you just learned to live with them as though they're part of your life, when really, just below the surface, a rich landscape of lost experience is waiting to be unearthed.

By exploring your core complaint, and listening to the language of your body, you're likely to uncover what may be keeping you locked in suffering.

If you're struggling with a physical symptom, answer these questions: Where do you experience it? Where's it located in your body? What sensations are you aware of? Mark them on the chart below.

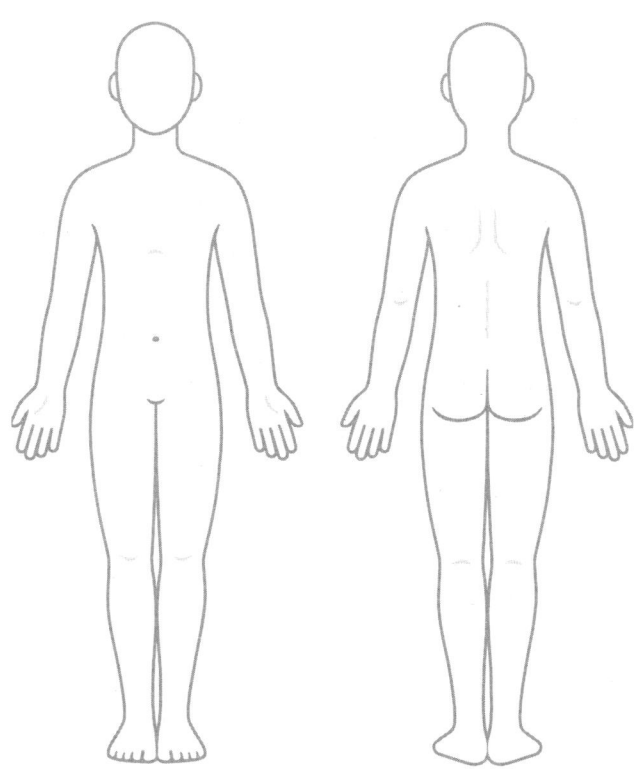

What emotions come up as you think about your symptom?

....
....
....

If that symptom or condition or part of your body had a message for you, what might it be saying to you?

....
....
....

How might your symptom be trying to protect you? Is it keeping you tight? Braced? Contracted? Numb? Disconnected? Invisible? Susan's shoulder was bracing as though to carry the weight of the world. How might your symptom be trying to serve you?

....
....
....
....
....

Now read what you've written. You may have just uncovered some of the nonverbal ways your core complaint is operating in your body.

DIGGING DEEPER: UNEARTHING THE CORE LANGUAGE IN OUR CORE COMPLAINT

Sometimes, the core language of our core complaint is so compelling, it forces us to excavate the family burial ground for answers. Yet the history we seek may not be readily available. Masked in shame, pushed away in pain, or protected in the form of a family secret, this information is unlikely to be talked about at the dinner table.

Other times, we may know the traumatic history of our family, but we don't yet see the link to our present experiences.

The core language of your core complaint can guide you like a compass through generations of unexplained family angst. There, a traumatic event may be waiting to be remembered and explored, so that it can finally be laid to rest.

> ## Common Themes Connecting Core Complaints to Family History
>
> Here are some themes I've observed that repeat in families. Do you recognize any of them in your family?
>
> - **Language that repeats:** Is there language that doesn't seem to fit in the context of your life experience? If so, could this language belong to someone in your family?

- **Ages that repeat:** Is there a connection between the age you were when your symptom or problem first appeared and the age of a family member when they struggled or suffered? If, for example, you had a parent who died young, you could develop an issue or symptom that limits your life in some way when you reach the same age as that parent. Unconsciously, it might be difficult for you to be happy or live fully beyond the age when he or she died. Your problem or symptom can even begin when your child reaches the same age that you were when your parent died. In a similar vein, your child can express a fear or symptom at the same age you were when you experienced something difficult. Children often mirror to us as parents what we felt at their age, but have long ago suppressed. It's almost as if they're saying, *"Mommy, this is what you felt at my age. You blocked it, so I'm showing it to you so it can finally heal."*

- **Events that repeat:** Sometimes fear, anxiety, or another symptom strikes unexpectedly when we reach a certain milestone in our lives. We get married or have a child. We get rejected by our partner or move away from our parents' home. Then suddenly, as though there's an ancestral alarm clock that starts ringing inside us, a symptom appears. When this happens, we have to ask ourselves, did someone in our family suffer or struggle when they experienced a similar event?

- **Emotions, behaviors, and symptoms that repeat:** Think back. What triggered your problem or symptom? What was happening in the background? Did someone leave you? Did you feel slighted, rejected, or abandoned? Did something happen that made you feel like you wanted to give up or quit? Does your issue or symptom mimic or recreate a certain experience or situation from your early childhood? Is it similar in any way to an event in your family history? Does it resemble anything that happened to your mother, father, grandmother, or grandfather?

EXERCISE

TWELVE QUESTIONS THAT GENERATE CORE LANGUAGE

If you don't yet see a connection between your core complaint and what you know about your family history, the following is a list of questions that can help you unearth some of your core language. Answer each question in as much detail as possible. Keep an open mind. Don't edit your responses. The answers to these questions can illuminate a connection between a current issue and a trauma in your family history.

What was taking place in your life when your symptom or problem first appeared?

....
....
....

What was going on right before it started?

....

What were you most worried about at the time?

....

What were you afraid would happen to you?

....

What age were you when the symptom or problem first appeared?

....

Did something traumatic happen to someone in your family at a similar age?

....

What exactly happens when you experience the problem?

....

What does it feel like in its worst moments?

....

What happens right before you feel this way or have the symptom?

....

What makes it better or worse?

....

What does the problem or symptom keep you from being able to do? What does it force you to do?

....

If the feeling or symptom never went away, what would be the worst thing that could happen to you?

....

Now that you've considered all the ways your core complaint might be expressing itself, let's put it all together here.

My core complaint is . . .

....
....

....

....

....

Now read what you've written.

Listen for words that have a strong emotional charge.

Listen for words that have a dramatic or urgent quality.

Listen for words that might not fit in context to your life experience. For example: "I'll be sent away. I'll be forgotten. I won't deserve to live."

Look for symptoms and behaviors that appear at a certain age.

Look for symptoms and behaviors that show up after a particular event.

The answers to these questions can reveal significant clues to unearthing a family connection.

COMPLAINTS AND SYMPTOMS AS CLUES FOR RESOLUTION

When looked at out of the box, your complaint or symptom can be a creative expression leading you to complete something, heal something, integrate something, or separate from something—perhaps a feeling you've taken on that never belonged to you in the first place.

Perhaps your symptom or issue is forcing you to take a step you haven't taken, a step you can no longer ignore. Maybe you are being asked to complete a stage in your development that got interrupted when you were small. Maybe your symptom or issue recreates a childlike state of helplessness that brings you closer to your parents. Or conversely, maybe your symptom or issue forces growth and independence from them.

Maybe you are being shown that you need to finish a task or follow a path you abandoned. Maybe you have ignored a young, fragmented part of yourself that expresses in symptoms, and now, that young part of you needs your attention and care. Maybe you neglected a personal boundary that can no longer remain overlooked.

I once worked with a man, a self-described "giver" and "people-pleaser," who complained that he had no energy. His posture was slouched. His head dipped forward as if his neck couldn't support its weight. He told me that he was exhausted all the time. "Running on empty," he said.

When looked at out of the box, his exhaustion revealed to him that, by living outside himself to please others, he had depleted himself inside. The symptom was merely serving to amplify what was already there.

On another level, "exhaustion" was just the excuse he needed to stop taking care of others. His symptom was functioning as a boundary, giving him the space he was never able to take for himself.

Our symptoms and complaints can also lead us to mend a broken relationship or help us to heal a personal trauma by forcing us to confront feelings we long ago suppressed. Not only can they give us insight into a family trauma that was never fully resolved, they can also give us insight into a personal guilt we carry, perhaps even lighting the path toward reconciliation.

How might your symptom or complaint be trying to communicate with you? What is it asking you to do or look at?

....
....
....

What is it asking you to complete, heal, integrate, or separate from?

....
....
....

If your symptom or complaint were guiding you to examine a feeling or emotion you've ignored, or deal with a situation you've been reluctant to confront, what feeling, emotion, or situation would that be?

....
....
....

How might your complaint or symptom be moving you toward healing?

....
....
....

Our complaints, symptoms, and problems can function as signposts pointing us in the direction of something that's still unresolved. They can help bring something to light that we cannot see, or connect us with something or someone that we, or our family, have rejected. When we stop and explore them, what's unresolved can rise to the surface, adding a new dimension to our healing process. We can emerge feeling more whole and complete.

Now that you've captured your core complaint, let's take a look at your core descriptors.

CHAPTER 5

YOUR CORE DESCRIPTORS

The feelings we hold about our parents are a doorway into ourselves. They are also a doorway into the four unconscious themes introduced in chapter 3, helping us pinpoint which ones are operating in our lives.

Your *core descriptors* refer to the way you describe your biological mother and father, which I'll ask you to do shortly. In doing so, let yourself be free with your responses. As you move through the following exercises, you are likely to discover more about yourself than about your parents.

If you've never met your biological parents, or don't have any information or stories about them, then proceed to the next chapter.

 **EXERCISE**

DESCRIBE YOUR MOTHER

Take a moment to describe your mother—the mother you remember from your earliest memories. What was she like? What adjectives or phrases instantly come to mind? Was she warm? Loving? Cold? Distant? Happy? Sad? Did she hug you a lot, or rarely hug you? How would you describe the love you got from her?

Also answer this: How would your mother describe the love she got from *her* mother? If she didn't get a lot of love, that could have affected the love you received and ultimately the way you describe her.

Write everything down. Don't do this in your head. It's essential that you write down the words as they come to you.

....
....
....

My mother would describe the love she got from her mother as . . .

....

....

....

Also, write down what you blame your mother for, if anything.

I blame her for . . .

....

....

....

EXERCISE

DESCRIBE YOUR FATHER

Now, take a moment to describe your father—the father you remember from your earliest memories. Was he kind? Easygoing? Harsh? Critical? Was he involved or not involved? How would your father describe the love he got from his mother?

Again, write everything down. Resist the impulse to edit.

....
....
....

My father would describe the love he got from his mother as . . .

....

....

....

Also, write down what you blame him for, if anything.

I blame my father for . . .

....

....

....

EXERCISE

DESCRIBE YOUR CURRENT OR MOST RECENT PARTNER

While you're in the flow, describe your current romantic partner, if you have one. If not, describe the last partner you had. If this relationship was in the past, let yourself experience it as if it were happening now. Is this person loving or distant? Available or unavailable? Supportive of your needs or self-absorbed? Also describe how you experience yourself in this relationship. Do you feel seen or unseen? Valued or unappreciated? Do you feel your partner makes you a priority, or do you feel invisible?

My partner is . . .

....

....

....

I blame him or her for . . .

....

....

....

I experience myself in this relationship as being . . .

....

....

....

Now let's take a look at what has just been revealed in your writing. I call these spontaneous, off-the-cuff adjectives and phrases *core descriptors*. These descriptors are a doorway into our unconscious feelings. They can reveal feelings about our parents that we might not even be aware we hold.

Writing down an impromptu list of adjectives and phrases gives us the opportunity to bypass the adult-rationalized, refined version of our childhood story. In this exercise, our true attitudes can emerge devoid of the usual filters and censors. This list can put us in touch with unconscious loyalties and alliances we share with our parents. What's more, it can reveal how we have rejected one or both of our parents, or how we have adopted the very behaviors we judge as negative in them. These descriptors don't lie, because they come from an inner image we carry, an image we formed long ago, perhaps to protect ourselves from feeling hurt. When we were small, our bodies functioned as recorders chronicling the information we took in and storing it as feeling states. The adjectives we use to describe our parents take us back into these feeling states and the images that accompany them.

Many of us hold images that are painful: images of our parents not giving us enough, images of not getting what we needed. Unchecked, these inner images can direct the course of our lives, forming a blueprint for how our lives will continue. These images are also incomplete. An essential truth is missing. What traumatic events lurk behind these images that were powerful enough to derail the flow of love in our family?

> **Susan described her** mother as a great mom and a great friend. "She stayed at home with my sister and me. She led our Girl Scout troops, attended every field trip and event, and planned the most amazing birthday parties. She was outgoing. People really loved her."
>
> Then Susan said, "I remember her as always there, but always busy. Even though she did all the right things, she wasn't emotionally present, and I never felt safe sharing my feelings with her. If I was crying, I would stop my

tears before she saw me. If I felt sad, I would hide. I never wanted her attention on me, especially when I was upset."

"Tell me more about what her attention felt like physically in your body," I said.

"It felt like she was way too close, almost like she was crawling inside me."

I wondered what would make closeness with her mother feel so terrible. "Tell me about the love your mom got from her mom. How would your mom have described it?"

"I think she would say Grandma was distant and disconnected." Susan added, "I do know that my grandmother's mother died in childbirth when she was two, so my grandmother never really knew her mom."

Bingo. Now Susan's core descriptors about her mother had a context. When Susan described her resistance to her mother's care, I suspected there was an attachment trauma. But how far back did it go? Such a massive trauma lurking in the background set the stage for a feeling of motherlessness that would be experienced for three generations.

Susan's core descriptors of mother: outgoing, great friend to others, always there but always busy, not emotionally present, felt way too close—like "she was crawling inside me"

How Susan's mother experienced love from her mother: distant and disconnected

When we've had a close relationship with our parents, our core descriptors reveal the warmth and compassion we feel toward them. When we feel positive toward our parents, we tend to feel positive about life, and trust that good things will continue to come our way.

If we had a difficult relationship with our parents, our core descriptors will expose the resentments we're still harboring. When we're resentful, it erodes our inner peace. Those of us who feel that we didn't receive enough from our parents, especially from our mothers, often feel that we don't receive enough from life.

Sometimes our core descriptors reveal mixed feelings. In most cases, people hold disparate feelings toward their parents, yet one theme or essential thread of core language often stands out as unresolved. And this is what we're looking for. For some of us, the actions of our parents are still felt as personal attacks or rejections, which can show up in what we blame them for.

Based on the core descriptors you've written, are there resentments or accusations you still hold toward your parents?

....

....

....

Do these resentments and accusations show up in your core descriptors of your partner?

....

Often, our discontent toward our parents gets projected onto our partner. What is unresolved with our parents does not automatically disappear. It serves as a template that forges our later relationships.

As we saw in Susan's story, our feelings often get projected in our intimate relationships. For example, if we felt unseen by our mother, we may feel invisible to our partner. If we felt our mother was too busy for us, we may not feel that we're a priority with our partner. If our mother was cold or distant, we may experience our partner as cold. But is that the truth? Could it be that our perspective is skewed?

It's as though we're looking with an eye that sees only the past, and we can't see the facts of the present. To protect ourselves from being hurt again, we focus on the negative traits, for if we were to acknowledge the positive, the rug could be swept out from under us, and we could tumble into darkness again.

COMMON CORE DESCRIPTORS FROM A BREAK IN THE BOND

There are many of us who experienced a physical or emotional separation from our mother and struggle to find peace, that feeling of solid ground beneath our feet. The following are some common core descriptors from people who experienced an early disconnection from their mothers:

> ▶ "Mom was cold and distant. She never held me. I didn't trust her at all."

- "My mother was too busy for me. She never had any time for me."
- "My mom and I are really close. She's like a little sister I take care of."
- "My mom was weak and fragile. I was much stronger than she was."
- "I don't ever want to be a burden to my mom."
- "My mother was distant, emotionally unavailable, and critical."
- "She would always push me away. She doesn't really care about me."
- "We really don't have a relationship."
- "I felt much closer to my grandmother. She was the one who mothered me."
- "My mother is completely self-centered. It's all about her. She never showed me any love."
- "She can be very calculating and manipulative. I didn't feel safe with her."
- "I was scared of her. I never knew what was going to happen next."
- "I'm not close with her. She's not maternal—not like a mother."
- "I've never wanted children. I've never had that maternal feeling inside me."

Remember Susan's core descriptors of her mother as being "busy" and "emotionally unavailable"? These were my first clues that we were dealing with a break in the bond.

Note that not everyone who has experienced a break in the bond will be resentful toward his or her mother. Often the mother is deeply loved and trusted. Sometimes, after such a break, a child unknowingly shuts down to receiving the mother's nurturance, and instead attempts to take care of the mother as a way of bonding with her. Sometimes the break occurred so early in life that there is no cognitive memory of the disconnection. Body memories of the separation can be triggered, however, when we bond or feel someone pull away in a relationship. Without ever understanding why, we can feel overwhelmed by feelings of terror, dissociation, numbness, defeat, and annihilation.

Once again, it is essential that we make peace with our parents. Even if we can only do so inwardly. Healing with them not only brings us inner peace, it also allows for harmony to flow in the generations that follow. By softening toward our parents and dropping the story that stands in the way, we are more likely to halt the senseless repetition of generational suffering. While at first this might seem challenging (or even impossible), I have witnessed again and again the unexpected rewards of healing our connection with our parents, including positive outcomes in our health, relationships, and productivity.

Examining your core descriptors is a valuable step in rebuilding your relationship with your parents. It makes no difference whether your parents are living or have passed away; once you decrypt your core descriptors, the negative feelings, attitudes, and judgments you hold toward them can finally shift. Remember, the greater the emotional charge in your words, the deeper your pain. There is often sadness hibernating beneath your angry words. The sadness won't kill you. The anger actually might.

The image you have of your parents can affect the quality of the life you live. The good news is that this inner image, once revealed, can change. **You can't change your parents, but you can change the way you hold them inside you.** One of the keys to that change is in the next step: your core sentence.

CHAPTER 6

YOUR CORE SENTENCE

If you struggle with a fear or phobia, panic attacks, or obsessive thoughts, you know only too well what it feels like to be held captive in the prison of your inner life. The hard time you do inside yourself—the constant worry, the overwhelming emotions, the unnerving body sensations—can feel like a life sentence, yet no trial or conviction has ever taken place. Fear and anxiety shrink your world and drain your vitality, restricting the day in front of you and limiting the life ahead of you. It can be exhausting to live that way.

Finding a way out is simpler than you think. You just need to "do time" with a different kind of "life sentence"—the sentence that your worst fear creates. This sentence has probably been with you since you were a small child. Whether spoken aloud or said silently, this sentence deepens your despair. Yet at the same time, it can lead you out beyond your prison gates into a new world of understanding and resolution.

This sentence is called your *core sentence*. If the core language map is a tool for locating buried treasure, the core sentence is the diamond you find when you get there.

IDENTIFYING YOUR CORE SENTENCE

Before we go further, answer this question: If your life fell apart, if things went terribly wrong, what's your worst fear? What's the worst thing that could happen to you? It's probably a fear or feeling you've had your whole life. You might even feel as though you were born with it. Write it down.

My worst fear, the worst thing that could happen to me, is . . .

....

What you've just written is your core sentence. Don't read further until you've written it down.

Maybe your core sentence begins with the word "I": "I would lose everything."

Maybe it begins with the word "They": "They would destroy me."

Maybe it begins with the word "My": "My children/family/wife/husband would leave me."

A core sentence can begin with many other words as well. Now let's go deeper and answer the same question again. This time, don't edit. Keep writing until you've gone as far as you can go.

The worst thing that could happen to me is . . .

"I . . ."

"They . . ."

"I could . . ."

"My children/family/spouse could . . ."

....

....

....

....

....

Now look at what you've written. If you think you've reached the bottom, ask yourself one more question: And if that happened, then what? What would be the worst part of that?

For example, if you wrote the sentence "I could die," take

it a bit further. And if that happened, what would be the worst part of that?

"My family would be without me."

Go one more level down. And what would be the worst part of that? "They'll forget me."

Can you feel how the sentence "They'll forget me" has a bit more juice than the previous two sentences?

Take another moment to narrow down and deepen the emotional resonance of your core sentence.

My absolute worst fear is . . .

....

Now let's look again at the words you've written. Your core sentence probably contains three, four, maybe five or six words. As I mentioned earlier, it is frequently an "I" or a "They" sentence, but it can start with other words as well. Often it's a sentence that's stated in the present or future tense, as though either it's happening right now or it's just about to happen. The words feel alive inside you. They resonate in your body when spoken aloud. When the core sentence is on target, it hits more like a ping on crystal than a thud on wood. Core sentences sound like this:

"I'm all alone."   *"I'll lose everything."*
"They reject me."   *"I'll fall apart."*
"They leave me."   *"It's all my fault."*
"I let them down."   *"They abandon me."*

"They betray me."
"They humiliate me."
"I'll go crazy."
"I'll hurt my child."
"I'll lose my family."
"I'll lose control."
"I'll do something terrible."
"I'll hurt someone."
"I won't deserve to live."
"I'll be hated."
"I'll kill myself."
"They'll lock me up."
"They'll put me away."
"It'll never end."

There's one more step. If you wrote down a sentence like "I'm all alone," inch the dial in both directions to make sure your core sentence pings at its highest-possible frequency.

For example, is your sentence "I'm all alone," or is it more like "They leave me"? Is it "They leave me" or is it more like "They reject me" or "They abandon me"?

The same way your optometrist checks and double-checks your vision for your prescription, you're checking to make sure the words align exactly with the feeling inside you. Keep testing it. Is your core sentence more like "They abandon me" or "I'm abandoned"? Your body will know which words are best by the vibration that's created inside you. The right words of your core sentence create a physical reaction—often an anxious or sinking feeling—when they are spoken.

My core sentence is . . .

....

....

....

Susan shared her core descriptors of her mother. Now I wanted to hear her core sentence. I asked her, "What's your worst fear? What's the worst thing that could happen to you?"

"I'll be annihilated," she answered instantly. "I don't know why, but I've felt that way my entire life."

Can you feel the emotional "juice" of such a sentence? It's palpable. I thought about Susan's description of her mother's attention "crawling inside her" and knew she was describing a break in the bond—the feeling of not trusting her mother's care.

There are a number of scenarios that can create the sentence "I'll be annihilated," and more often than not, it stems from the womb. If our mother, while she was pregnant with us, had a significant trauma, this could be our sentence. Maybe she conceived us out of wedlock. Or she wasn't going to keep us. Or our father left her while she was pregnant, or he had an affair.

In Susan's case, her mother lost two babies before her. Fearful of losing the next baby, Susan's mother would have had no idea of the effects that her fears would have on Susan. With stress hormones flooding the placenta, clouding her connection with her mother, Susan would have felt as though her very life were in danger. For Susan, the core sentence "I'll be annihilated" was the muffled cry of a fetus experiencing extreme distress in the womb.

Susan's core sentence: "I'll be annihilated."

TYPES OF CORE SENTENCES

With your core sentence fine-tuned, can you tell whose story is being told? Yours or someone else's? Can you hear clues in the language? Is this sentence leading you back to an early trauma you had with your mother or to a generational wound?

For example, let's say your core sentence is "I'll be helpless and powerless." At what age do people generally feel helpless and powerless? Fetuses, infants, and toddlers who are unable to protect themselves from something overwhelming or from someone hurtful—they feel helpless and powerless. If this is your core sentence, did you experience a break in the attachment with your mother?

Take this sentence: "I'll be hated by everyone." Notice it has a different quality than the previous core sentence. It's the sentence of someone older. Perhaps someone who was hated in the family. Or someone who did something, or was perceived as having done something, that caused (or could have caused) his or her expulsion from the family or community.

A common scenario that creates this type of core sentence is this: Our mother or father or grandmother or grandfather had an affair, or multiple affairs, or left the family, or lost the family's money. Their actions evoked the ire of those who suffered because of what they did. You can feel the difference in this sentence. It has a generational undertone. Someone in the past did something hurtful, and now, unconsciously aligned with them, we're carrying the consequences of their actions, the feeling that we'll be hated. Below is a list of common core sentences. Can you distinguish whether the words of your core sentence reflect an attachment trauma or a generational trauma?

Attachment Trauma Core Sentences

I'll be all alone.	I won't matter.
I'll be abandoned.	I won't exist.
I'll be rejected.	I'll lose everything.
I'll be left.	I'll fall apart.
I'll lose control.	I'll lose my family.
I'll be helpless.	I'll be betrayed.
I'll be powerless.	I'll be ridiculed.
I'll be homeless.	I'll be judged.
I'll be annihilated.	I'll be humiliated.
I'll be destroyed.	

Generational Trauma Core Sentences

I'll lose everything.	I'll go crazy.
I'll fall apart.	They'll lock me up.
I'll hurt someone.	I'll lose my family.
I'll let someone down.	I'll do something terrible.
It'll all be my fault.	I won't deserve to live.
I'll be hated.	I'll lose control.
I'll be ostracized.	I'll kill somebody.
I'll be sent away.	I'll hurt a child.
I'll be forgotten.	I'll take my life.

Does your core sentence resonate more with attachment trauma or generational trauma? Or do you hear hints of both?

....

....

....

OTHER PATHS TO FINDING YOUR CORE SENTENCE

If you tried to write your core sentence and nothing came to you, then answer this question: What's the worst thing that could happen to someone? Someone else. Not you. Perhaps you remember a news story of something terrible that happened to somebody you didn't know. Or maybe something awful happened to somebody you did know. What was it? Write it down. What you remember is important. It might even say something about you.

What's the worst thing that could happen to someone else?

....

....

....

Many times, another's tragedy reflects a facet of our own worst fears. Of the myriad painful images around us, those that strike a familiar chord, or to be more exact, a *familial* chord, tend to resonate with us. Call it a back door into the family psyche. Of all the terrible things that happen to people, the one that strikes us as the most terrible will likely link to a traumatic event in our own family system. It can also remind us of a trauma we personally experienced. When another's tragedy resonates with us, there is generally something about that tragedy that belongs to us on some level.

EXCAVATING THE ORIGIN OF YOUR CORE SENTENCE

A core sentence often invokes feelings and sensations of fear. Just by speaking its words, we can experience a strong physical reaction in our bodies. Many people report waves of sensation reverberating inside them as the sentence is spoken. We may be the one speaking the core sentence and carrying its fears, but the original fear can stem from a tragic event that took place long before we were even born. The question we ask is: To whom does the initial fear belong?

Say your core sentence to yourself. Feel its vibration inside. Listen inwardly. Imagine for a moment that the words belong to someone else. You may even want to write your core sentence down again to see the words in front of you.

My core sentence is . . .

....

When I say it, my body feels . . .

....

....

....

I'm aware of these sensations in these areas of my body:

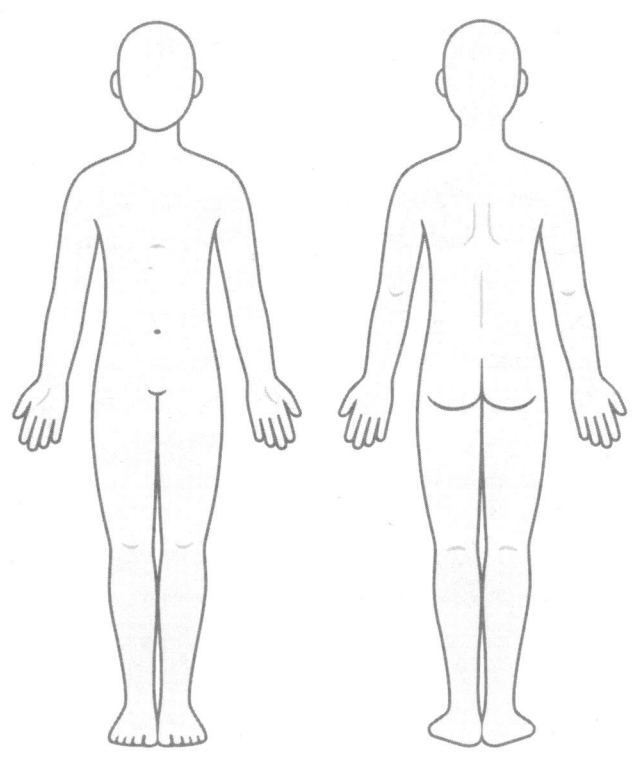

Even though you may feel this sentence vibrate in your body, it might belong to someone else, someone who experienced a great trauma, or carried deep grief or guilt, or died violently, or lived a life of emptiness or quiet desperation. This sentence could be the sentence of your mother or your father. It could belong to your grandmother or grandfather, or even to your older sibling or to an uncle or aunt. And now it lives on in you.

Core sentences are traveling sentences, much like traveling salesmen, who knock on door after door until someone lets them in. But the doors they solicit are the psyches of those who follow in a family system. And the invitation to enter is without conscious permission.

These sentences affect the way you know yourself. They affect the choices you make. They affect how your mind and body respond to the world around you. Imagine the effect of a sentence like "He'll leave me" playing out in the back of your awareness when the man of your dreams proposes. Or consider the impact of a sentence like "I'll hurt my child" on the complex biological and emotional state of a young mother-to-be.

Listen again to the words of your core sentence. Speak them aloud.

Are you sure they're your words? If not, who in your family might have had cause to feel the same way?

Think of your parents and your grandparents. Did they experience an event so painful that they rarely spoke about it? Did they lose a newborn baby or miscarry late in a pregnancy? Were they abandoned by a great love or did they lose a parent or a sibling when they were young? Did they feel guilty for causing harm to someone? Did they blame themselves for something?

If nothing comes to mind, you might look back another generation to your great-grandparents, or to an uncle or aunt.

> **Jordan's core sentence** was closely related to his core complaint. When I asked him to share his worst fear, or the worst thing that could happen to him, he answered, "I'll do something terrible and harm someone I care about, and it will all be my fault."
>
> He had the words, but he still didn't know where they came from. As you'll learn in the next chapter, a tragic event lived in Jordan's family history—his *core trauma*.
>
> **Jordan's core sentence:** "I'll do something terrible and harm someone I care about, and it will all be my fault."

We appear to share an unconscious obligation to resolve the tragedies of our family's past. Even if you don't have any information about what happened in your family, the path toward healing is still straightforward. You've already done the hard part: you've isolated your deepest fear. Although you might carry the feelings of that fear, the fear itself likely originates in a traumatic event that occurred before you were born. Even if you don't know what it is, you can tell it's there. You feel it.

PRACTICE
ACKNOWLEDGING THE FAMILY MEMBER(S) BEHIND YOUR CORE SENTENCE

If you have a clear idea of the original owner of the fear expressed in your core sentence, visualize that person now.

If you are not clear who this person is, close your eyes. Imagine somebody in your family who might have felt similar emotions. This person might be your uncle or your grandmother or even the older half sibling you never met. You don't have to know who it is. This person might not even be a blood member of your family, but may have harmed someone or been harmed by someone in your family.

Visualize the person or people connected to the traumatic event behind your core sentence. You don't even need to know what that event is. Now bow your head and breathe deeply. Exhale with your mouth slightly open.

Tell this person or these people that you respect them and all that happened to them. Tell them that they will not be forgotten and that they will be remembered with love.

Visualize them being at peace.

Feel them blessing you to have a full life. Feel their well wishes having a physical effect on your body as you breathe in. As you breathe out, feel the emotions of your core sentence leaving your body. Feel the fear dissipating as though the intensity dial were turned all the way down to zero.

Do this for several minutes, until your body quiets.

YOUR CORE SENTENCE: THE PATH TO TRANSFORMING FEAR

Of all the core language tools you learn in this book, the sentence that describes your worst fear, your core sentence, is the most direct path to uncovering unresolved family trauma. The core sentence not only guides you to the source of your fear, but it also connects you to the feelings of unresolved family trauma that might still live in your body. With the source in sight, the fear can begin to lift.

The Core Sentence: Eleven Key Attributes

1. It often links to a traumatic event in your family history or in childhood.
2. It frequently begins with an "I" or "They" sentence.
3. It has very few words, yet it's dramatic.
4. It contains the emotionally charged language of your greatest fear.
5. It causes a physical reaction when spoken.
6. It can retrieve the "lost language" of a trauma and help you locate where this language originated in your family history.

7. It can recover trauma memories that could not be integrated.
8. It can help you discern whether you struggle with an attachment trauma or a generational trauma.
9. It can provide you with a context for understanding the emotions, sensations, and symptoms you've been experiencing.
10. It targets the cause, not the symptoms.
11. It has the power, when spoken, to release you from the past.

You've now gathered all the core language you need to take the fourth and final step—uncovering the core trauma in your family.

CHAPTER 7

YOUR CORE TRAUMA

Let's put all the pieces of our core language map together. So far, we've learned to extract the core language gems from our core complaint. We've learned how to analyze our core descriptors, how the adjectives we use to describe our parents often say more about us than they do about them. We've also learned that the sentence that expresses our greatest fear, our core sentence, can lead us back to a trauma in our childhood or family system. The last thing we need to learn is how to construct a bridge to get to our core trauma, the unresolved trauma in our childhood or family history.

There are two ways to unearth the core trauma. One is through a genogram, a diagram of our family tree. And the other is through a bridging question.

THE BRIDGING QUESTION

If you've tapped into the urgent language that expresses your deepest fear, but you're not sure where it comes from, a bridging question can summon forth the family member from whom you may have inherited it. Excavating the feelings of your greatest fear can lead you to the person in your family system who had cause to feel the same way you do. Because our core sentence may originate in a past generation, locating the rightful owner can bring about peace and understanding, not only for us, but for our children as well.

Simply put, a bridging question is a question that connects the present to the past. Return to your core sentence, and turn that fear into a question. Think about all the relevant combinations that could express in a fear carried by a descendant in the family.

For example, if your core sentence relates to harming a child:

- Was there a child in your family system who was harmed, neglected, given away, or mistreated?

- Who in your family system might have blamed himself or herself for hurting a child or not keeping a child safe?

- Who might have felt guilty for actions or decisions that harmed a child?

- Who might have held himself or herself responsible for a child's death?

EXERCISE

IDENTIFYING BRIDGING QUESTIONS FROM YOUR CORE SENTENCE

My core sentence is . . .

....

My bridging questions are . . .

....

....

....

....

One or more of these questions is likely to lead you to the source of your fear. However, the source might not always be readily available. Many parents and grandparents keep the family past tightly sealed, and thus, valuable information can be lost forever.

When people suffer deeply, they often attempt to distance themselves from their emotional pain by avoiding it. In this way, they think that they are protecting themselves and protecting their children. But ignoring the pain actually deepens it. What is hidden from sight often increases in intensity. Remaining silent about family pain is rarely an effective strategy for healing it. The suffering will surface again at a later time, often expressing in the fears or symptoms of a later generation.

Jordan had discovered his deepest fear with his core sentence: "I'll do something terrible and harm someone I care about, and it will all be my fault." Now it was time to discover where that fear came from.

He was in regular contact with both his parents, so I gave him some homework in the form of bridging questions:

- Who in the family might have blamed himself or herself for harming someone they cared about when they were seventeen?

- Who might have held himself or herself responsible for someone's death?

- Who might have felt guilty for actions or decisions that harmed someone they cared about?

- Was someone in the family harmed, given away, or mistreated at age seventeen?

- Who was harmed by someone in the family when they were seventeen—or when the family member was seventeen?

I reminded Jordan that his family system includes not only his blood relatives, but anyone who harmed or murdered or took advantage of a family member, as well as anyone harmed or murdered or taken advantage of by a family member.

When Jordan called his father, the mystery was solved with the very first question. "Did anyone in our family blame themselves for harming someone they cared about when they were seventeen?" Jordan asked.

His father was shocked. "How did you know that? My father—your grandfather—accidentally ran over his best friend with his truck when he was seventeen. He never spoke of it again. I heard about it from my aunt, who told me after he died. She said he was never the same after that—he never stopped blaming himself."

Unbeknownst to Jordan, he had been living the story of his grandfather—the utter horror of killing his best friend. How would his grandfather feel every time he got into his truck? How could he not see that image over and over again? *Oh my God, what have I done?* Through his epigenetic inheritance, Jordan carried that same horror.

Even if you can't find out what happened in your family, you can still complete your core language map. Your core sentence will provide you with the clues you need to point you in the direction of a family trauma. Your bridging question will connect enough of the dots, even if the specific details are vague or missing.

A bridging question is one way to discover the unresolved trauma in your family. Mapping out your family tree and constructing a genogram is the other.

THE GENOGRAM

A genogram is a two-dimensional visual representation of a family tree. It's a map. Each image leads us to the next image, even if we don't know exactly what we're looking for. By charting it out, we can illuminate a trail of suffering that extends from a tragic event preceding it.

Here are the steps to create your genogram:

1. Looking back three or four generations in your family, construct a diagram that includes your parents, grandparents, great-grandparents, siblings, uncles, and aunts. You don't need to go back any further than your great-grandparents. List the children of your parents, grandparents, and great-grandparents. You do not need to list the children of your aunts, uncles, or siblings. Using squares to represent males and circles to represent females, create your family tree. (See the diagram on page 142.) You can use lines to represent the branches of the family tree, showing who belongs in which generation. However you map this out will be fine.

2. Next to each family member, write down the significant traumas, catastrophic events, and hardships that person experienced. If your parents are still alive, you might ask them what they know. Don't worry if there are answers you can't get. Whatever you know should be enough.

As a reminder, traumatic events include: Who died early? Who left? Who was abandoned or isolated or excluded from the family? Who was adopted or who gave a child up for adoption? Who died in childbirth? Who had a stillbirth or an abortion? Who died by suicide? Who committed a crime? Who lost their home or possessions and had difficulty recovering? Who was forgotten or suffered in war? Who died in or participated in the Holocaust or another genocide? Who was murdered? Who murdered someone? Who felt responsible for someone's death or misfortune?

These questions are important. If someone in your family harmed or murdered someone, list the harmed or murdered person in your family tree. The victims harmed by people in your family must be included, as they are now members of your family system with whom you could be identified. Likewise, list anyone who harmed or murdered a member of your family, as you could also be unconsciously identified with this person.

Keep going. Who hurt, cheated, or took advantage of someone? Who profited from another's loss? Who was wrongly accused of something? Who was jailed or institutionalized? Who had a physical, emotional, or mental disability? Which parent or grandparent had a significant relationship prior to getting married, and what happened? List any significant former partners of your parents and grandparents. List anyone else you can think of who was deeply hurt by someone or deeply hurt another.

3. At the top of the genogram, write down your core sentence. Now look at everyone who belongs in your family system. Who might have had a reason to feel the same way you do? This person could be your mother or your father, especially if one of them had a difficult life or was disrespected by the other. It could also be the sister of your grandmother who was institutionalized, or the older brother that your mother miscarried before she had you. Often, it is someone who isn't talked about much in your family.

Take a look at the following example. This genogram tells the story of a woman named Ellie who struggled with a fear of going crazy. Until she constructed the maternal line of her genogram, Ellie believed that she was the source of that fear.

CORE SENTENCE: "I'LL GO CRAZY"

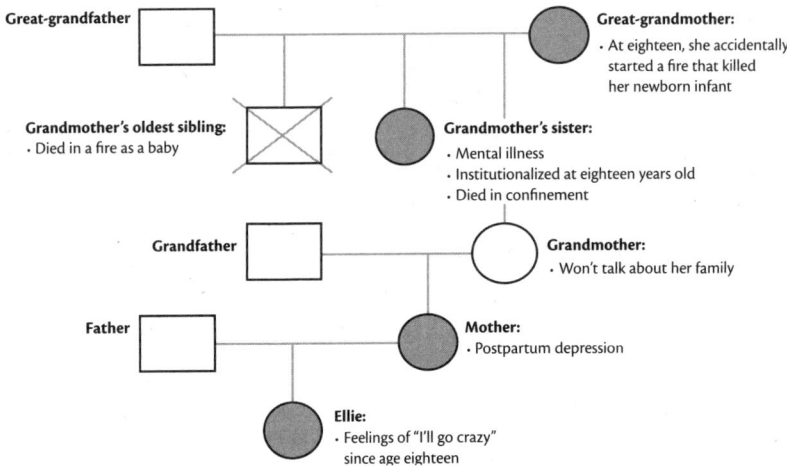

In the genogram, it's easy to see that the feeling of going crazy did not originate in the current generation with Ellie. Ellie's great-aunt was institutionalized at eighteen and died alone and forgotten. No one in the family ever spoke her name or told her story. Ellie never even knew that her grandmother had any siblings, and discovered the information only through repeated inquiries.

Interestingly, the great-aunt was committed to a state hospital at eighteen—the same age the great-grandmother was when she started a fire that killed her newborn child. With three generations in view, a new understanding for Ellie was possible. Whose feelings of insanity had the great-aunt been reliving? And more important, what story was Ellie trying to bring back to the forefront by sharing the same fear? With the genogram laid out, the fogged history of Ellie's family was now becoming clear.

For Ellie, the fear of going crazy arose once she turned eighteen and graduated from high school. The same fear that had been depleting her life force was now leading her toward self-discovery. The more she studied the genogram, the more connections she began to make.

Ellie remembered her mother telling her that she had experienced postpartum depression for the first year of Ellie's life. In her suffering, Ellie's mother was also a recipient of the great-grandmother's trauma. Ellie's mother admitted that, as soon as Ellie was born, she began obsessing that something would go terribly wrong. Specifically, she was terrified that she would inadvertently do something and, as a consequence, Ellie would die. Unbearable feelings of dread arose during the pregnancy and intensified after Ellie was born. Ellie's mother never connected the depression to what had happened in her family. What wasn't talked about consciously in the family was expressed unconsciously through the fears, feelings, and behaviors of its members.

 **EXERCISE**

CREATING YOUR GENOGRAM

For this exercise, use the genogram worksheet below. Using squares for males and circles for females, position the members of your family, along with the significant traumas and difficult fates they experienced. Write your core sentence at the top of the page.

CORE SENTENCE:

....

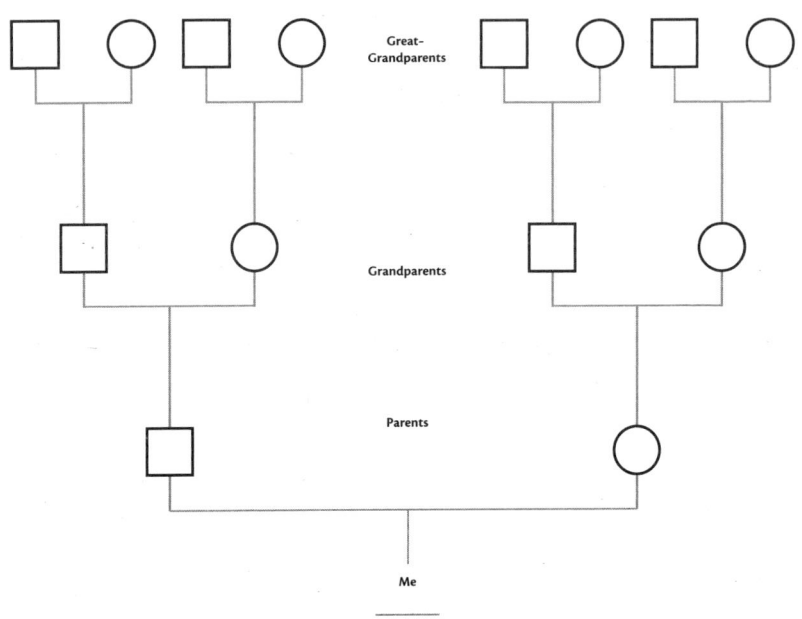

Now sit back and look at your genogram. Without focusing too carefully, let your eyes take in the whole gestalt. Absorb the energy on both sides of your family. Feel the quality of weight, the lightness or heaviness of the emotions, into which you were born. Compare your paternal line with your maternal line. Which side feels weightier? Which side has a more burdensome feeling? Look at the traumatic events. Who suffered the most difficult fate? Who lived the most difficult life? How did other family members feel about this person? Who or what was rarely talked about in your family? Don't worry if the information you have is incomplete. Let your thoughts, feelings, and body sensations be your guide.

Now speak your core sentence out loud. Who in the family would have echoed a similar feeling? Who would have struggled with similar emotions? Chances are your core sentence existed long before you were even born.

Susan constructed a genogram that looked like this:

CORE SENTENCE: "I'LL BE ANNIHILATED"

- Great-grandfather
- Great-grandmother:
  - Died giving birth to Grandma
- Grandmother's oldest sibling:
  - Died in war
- Grandfather
- Grandmother:
  - Distant and cold
- Mother's oldest sibling:
  - Died in war
- Father
- Mother
- Late-term miscarriage
- Late-term miscarriage
- Late-term miscarriage when Susan was two years old
- Susan's Sister:
  - Died at age thirty-nine of an overdose
- Susan

When we examine Susan's genogram, we can see that the core sentence "I'll be annihilated" began with Susan's grandmother, who spent nine months in her mother's womb and then suddenly lost her mother in childbirth. The shock and terror must have felt annihilating to her. This shock would likely be carried epigenetically, as altered DNA, downstream to Susan's mother, Susan, and Susan's sister.

For Susan, this terror of annihilation would be reengineered in her mother's womb. Having lost two babies before her, Susan's mother was sure Susan would die too. Fear, in the form of cortisol, flooded her womb, clouding the connection between her and her baby. Just like her grandmother, Susan would have felt the shock of being disconnected from her mother's warmth, care, and attunement. For her, it would have felt like there was no one there.

The Trail of Trauma

Feel the reverberations of your core sentence. Does it echo in your family history? Does it create a trail you can follow? If so, how far back does it go? Does it reach back to your grandparents or great-grandparents, or even beyond?

Look at the genogram again. What patterns do you notice?

As a reminder, here are some common ones:

Ages that repeat. Did any family members experience a trauma at a similar age? Maybe your grandfather died in a farming accident when he was forty-five, and your father died of cancer in his forties. Or your grandmother lost her husband at thirty-four, and your mother divorced in her mid-thirties. Maybe they both stayed alone after that, and you've been continuing that pattern of aloneness.

Events that repeat. Do you see a pattern of early deaths, broken marriages, suicides, or isolation? Maybe a child died in each generation at a similar age or similar position in the birth order.

Emotions, behaviors, and symptoms that repeat. Can you see a trail of similar illnesses; or emotions such as sadness, grief, guilt, or anger; or struggles such as incarceration or addiction that extend from generation to generation?

Can you find *your* core sentence in the stories of those who came before you?

Can you locate any other patterns?

Mark your genogram with a highlighter or a colored pen to show these trails of trauma.

When Susan expanded her genogram, she noticed another trail of trauma: a pattern of oldest sons who died in war. As she thought about it, she wondered if the pattern may have even extended to her sister, who died in the crossfire of the war on drugs.

Strangely, Susan's oldest son had always wanted to be in the military, to serve on the front line for the most dangerous assignments. He was now seventeen and preparing to enlist, despite being offered a college scholarship. Recognizing the pattern, Susan showed her son the genogram. She didn't tell him what to do, but simply allowed him to absorb it. Two weeks later, Susan's son approached her and said he had decided not to enlist. He accepted the scholarship and volunteered in his spare time as an EMT.

When I worked with Susan, I recognized she still had unresolved feelings surrounding the tragic overdose death of her younger sister. In one of our sessions together, I had her do the following practice. If you have a sibling who struggles deeply or who died, you might consider doing this practice as well.

PRACTICE

FOR A SIBLING WHO SUFFERS

If you have a sibling who struggles in life, maybe with addiction, or homelessness, or chronic illness—or who has died tragically—see this sibling in your mind's eye. Wherever they happen to be, whether they've passed away or they're alive, or they're living on the street or in your parents' house, tell them:

"Now, seeing our family history, I understand more. Thank you for carrying as much as you did. Because you took it on, I didn't have to. Because you suffered so deeply, I got to live more freely. I'm sorry if I judged you. Now I see what you did for our family, and I want to honor you for the pain you carry/carried."

Now visualize your sibling receiving these words. Breathe into your heart all the suffering they experienced, and then send out understanding and compassion and support to them. Do this several times until you feel they have received your love.

THE MAP HOME

By this point in the workbook, you've had the opportunity to gather the essential pieces of your core language map. You have likely discovered words or sentences you thought were yours but which may have, in fact, belonged to others. You have likely also made links in your family history, unearthing traumatic events or unspoken loyalties that seeded this language.

Now it's time to bring all the pieces together and take the next step. Here's a list of what you'll need:

- Your Core Complaint—the core language describing your worry, struggle, or complaint

- Your Core Descriptors—the core language describing your parents

- Your Core Sentence—the core language describing your worst fear

- Your Core Trauma—the event(s) in your family behind your core language

Based on your reflections so far, write down your core language map here:

My Core Complaint:

....

My Core Descriptors:

....

My Core Sentence:

....

My Core Trauma:

....

Your core language map is the torch lighting your way along your healing journey. With the connections you've just made, the only step remaining is to bring all that you have discovered back to yourself. What has been unspoken or invisible in your family history has likely been hidden in the shadows of your own self-awareness. Once you make it conscious, what was previously unseen becomes an opportunity for profound healing. Sometimes the new images that arise require our care and attention to integrate them fully. In the chapters that follow, I will guide you through exercises and give you practices and sentences that will strengthen these images so you can move toward greater wholeness and freedom.

But before we go there, let's connect a few of the dots.

EXERCISE

MAKING PEACE WITH YOUR FAMILY HISTORY

(If you've identified your issue as solely a break in the bond with your mother, and don't resonate with other traumatic events in the family history, you'll find what you're looking for in chapter 9.)

Write down the language of your core complaint or core sentence that has the greatest emotional charge or that evokes the most emotion in you when you speak it aloud.

....

Also write down your core trauma—the traumatic event or events connected to this core language.

....

List all the people whose lives were touched by this event. Who was the most affected? Your mother? Your father? A grandparent? An uncle? An aunt? Who isn't acknowledged or talked about? Is there a sibling who was given away or didn't survive? Did a grandparent or great-grandparent leave the family or die young or suffer in some terrible way? Was a parent or grandparent engaged or married previously? Is that former partner acknowledged in your family? Is there anyone outside your family who was judged, rejected, or blamed for harming a family member? Was there anyone in your family who harmed someone? Is the harmed person acknowledged?

....
....
....

Describe what happened. What images come to mind as you write? Take a minute and visualize what this person might have felt or gone through. What's happening in your body as you think about this?

....
....
....

Are there any family members you feel particularly drawn to? Do you feel yourself being pulled to them emotionally? Where in your body do you feel this? Is it a place you're familiar with? Do you experience sensitivity or symptoms in that same area?

....
....
....

Place your hand there and allow your breath to fill that area.

Visualize the family member or person(s) involved in this event. Tell them: "You are important. I will do something meaningful to honor you. I will make something good come out of this tragedy. I will live my life as fully as I can, knowing that this is what you want for me."

Construct your own personal language that acknowledges the unique connection you share with this person or these people.

....

....

....

CHAPTER 8

FROM INSIGHT TO INTEGRATION

Unconscious reliving can go on for generations. Once we recognize that we have been carrying thoughts, emotions, feelings, behaviors, or symptoms that do not originate with us, we can break the cycle. We start by taking a conscious action that acknowledges the tragic event and the people involved. Often this begins with a conversation we have internally, or with a family member—either in person or through visualization.

In chapters 9 and 10, you'll learn practices to heal a break in the bond with your mother, if you have one, as well as other traumas you may carry from your family history. But before I give you those practices, let me share some of the key elements and why they're so powerful. Those elements are healing sentences, resonant images, rituals, and experiences that can be felt in the body.

CREATING PERSONAL HEALING SENTENCES

In their book *Words Can Change Your Brain*, Dr. Andrew Newberg, a neuroscientist at Thomas Jefferson University Hospital, and his colleague Mark Robert Waldman write: "A single word has the power to influence the expression of genes that regulate physical and emotional stress."[1] They explain that just by concentrating on positive words, we affect areas of the brain that can improve our perception of ourselves and of the people we interact with.[2]

I've found that the right words can release us from the grip of an unconscious family loyalty and help us break the cycle of inherited trauma. The sentences below create new experiences inside us. Whether sentences of reconciliation or resolution, they can lead us to life-giving images and embodied sensations of well-being.

Examples of Healing Sentences

One man I worked with recognized that he had been unconsciously sharing his rejected grandfather's loneliness and isolation. He said these words: "I have been isolated and alone just like you. I can see that this doesn't even belong to me. I know this is not what you want for me. And I know it burdens you to see me suffer like this. From now on, I will live my life connected to the people around me. In this way, I'll honor you."

Another client understood that she had been unconsciously sharing the relationship failures and unhappiness of her mother and grandmother. She said these sentences: "Mom, please bless me to be happy with my husband, even though you couldn't be happy with Dad. To honor you and Dad, I will relish my love with my husband so that you both can see that things go well for me."

Another young woman shared with me that she'd been living in an anxious and contracted state for as long as she could remember. She said these words to her mother, who died while giving birth to her: "Every time I feel anxious, I will feel you smiling at me, supporting me, blessing me to be well. Whenever I feel my breath moving inside me, I will feel you there with me and know that you are happy for me."

Additional Healing Sentences

"Instead of reliving what happened to you, I promise to live my *own* life."

"What happened to you won't be in vain."

"I'll use what happened as a source of strength."

"I will honor the life you gave me by doing something good with it."

"I will do something meaningful and dedicate it to you."

"I will not leave you out of my heart."

"I'll light a candle for you."

"I will honor you by living fully."

"I'll live my life in a loving way."

"I will make something good come out of this tragedy."

"Now I understand. It helps to understand."

Do any of the above healing sentences resonate with you? If so, which one(s)? Who do you imagine saying it/them to?

HEALING SENTENCE THAT RESONATES	WHO I WOULD SAY IT TO

Can you come up with another healing sentence you might say?

....

....

....

HEALING IMAGES AND OUR BRAIN

Our minds have a vast capacity for healing through images. Whether we're imagining a scene of forgiveness, comfort, or letting go, or simply visualizing a loved one, images can profoundly settle into our bodies and sink into our minds.

In my work, I've found that helping people to unearth the image that most resonates with them is the cornerstone of healing.

Science supports this idea. Psychiatrist Norman Doidge revolutionized our understanding of how human brains operate by identifying a paradigm shift away from viewing the brain as fixed and unchanging to seeing it as flexible and capable of change. His work demonstrates how new experiences can create new neural pathways. These new neural pathways strengthen through repetition and deepen through focused attention. Essentially, the more we practice something, the more we train our brain to change. With enough repetition, it can become automatic.

We benefit most when we practice having a new experience we perceive as being positive, rewarding, or meaningful—one that engages our sense of curiosity and wonder. This can be an experience of receiving comfort or support, or feeling compassion or gratitude—ultimately anything that allows us to feel strength or peace inside.

When we repeatedly revisit the feelings and sensations associated with this new experience, not only can structures in our brain begin to wire together, but we can also stimulate the release of feel-good neurotransmitters, such as serotonin and dopamine, or feel-good hormones, such as oxytocin. Even how our genes express can be affected; the very genes involved in the body's stress response can begin to function in an improved way.

"You can't change your DNA," says Rachel Yehuda, a professor of psychiatry and neuroscience at New York University, "but if you can change the way your DNA functions, that's sort of the same thing."[3]

WHAT WE IMAGINE, WE MAKE POSSIBLE

When we make the link to the trauma behind our fears and symptoms, we are already opening up new possibilities for resolution. Sometimes the new understanding alone is enough to shift the old painful images we hold and initiate a visceral release that can be felt in the core of our body. In other cases, making the link increases understanding, but more is needed to fully integrate what we've learned. We will need sentences, rituals, practices, or exercises to help us forge a new inner image. The new image can fill us with a reservoir of calm, becoming an internal reference point of peace that we can return to again and again. With new thoughts, new feelings, new sensations, and new neural wiring, we begin to establish an inner experience of well-being that starts to compete with our old trauma reactions and their power to lead us astray.

A life completely devoid of trauma is highly unlikely. Traumas do not sleep even with death, but rather continue to look for the fertile ground of resolution in the children of the following generations. Fortunately, human beings are resilient and are capable of healing most types of trauma. This can happen at any time during our lives. We just need the right insights and tools.

Whether we're conscious of it or not, our life is profoundly influenced by the inner images, beliefs, expectations, assumptions, and opinions we hold. Intrinsic imprints such as "life never works out for me" or "I'll fail no matter what I try" or "I have a weak immune system" can lay a blueprint for how our life unfolds, limiting the way we take in new experiences and affecting the way we heal. Imagine the effect on your body of the inner image "my childhood was difficult." Or the image "my mother was cruel." Or "my father was emotionally abusive."

Although there may be a significant amount of truth in these images, they might not reveal the whole story. Was every day of your childhood difficult? Was your father ever gentle? Was your mother ever caring? Do you have access to all your early memories of being held, fed, and tucked into your crib at night when you were an infant?

Many of us hold on to only those memories designed to protect us from being hurt again, memories that support our defenses, memories that evolutionary biologists claim are part of our inborn "negativity bias." Could any memories be missing? More importantly, have you asked the questions: What was behind my mom's hurtfulness? What traumatic event lay behind my father's frustration? Questions like these take things out of the realm of what's personal so we can expand our vision of what's possible.

FROM NEW IMAGES TO NEW EXPERIENCES

Beginning in the next chapter, we're going to create new experiences through images, rituals, exercises, and practices. All of these can have a potent effect on healing. Essentially, they allow us to establish a feeling of wholeness, a reference point we can refer back to each time old feelings threaten our stability. These new experiences function much like new memories accompanied with new understandings, new feelings, and new sensations in the body. They can be powerful enough to overshadow the old, limiting images that have been running our lives.

Examples of Rituals, Exercises, Practices, and Healing Images

▶ **Placing a Photo on the Desk:** A man who understood that he had been reexperiencing his grandfather's guilt placed a photo of his grandfather on his desk. He breathed out and visualized leaving the guilt with his grandfather. Each time he repeated this ritual, he felt lighter and freer.

If you were to place a photo of someone on your desk or nightstand, who might that be?

....

....

....

▶ **Lighting a Candle:** A woman whose father died when she was an infant had no memory of him. Estranged from her husband at twenty-nine—the same age her father was when he died—she unconsciously shared her father's disconnection from the family. She lit a candle every night for two months and imagined the flame from the candle burning an opening for the two of them to reunite. She would speak to her father and feel his presence comforting her. Eventually her feelings of disconnection eased, and a new feeling of being cared for by a loving father expanded inside her.

If you were speaking to someone through the flame of a candle, what would you say?

....

....

....

▶ **Writing a Letter:** A man who had abruptly left his college fiancée found himself still struggling in his relationships twenty years later. He had learned that his fiancée had died the year after he left. Although he knew she would never receive his letter, he wrote to her, apologizing for his carelessness and indifference. In the letter, he said: "I'm so sorry. I know how much you loved me, and how much I hurt you. It must have been so terrible for you. I'm so very sorry. I know I'll never be able to deliver this letter, but I hope you will receive my words." After writing this letter, the man felt a sense of peace and completion.

If you were going to write a letter, to whom would you write it and what would you say?

....

....

....

- **Placing a Photo Above the Bed:** A woman who had spent her life rejecting her mother realized that an early separation in an incubator had kept her feeling suspicious and shut down to her mother's love. She also began to see how pushing her mother away had become a blueprint for pushing other relationships away. She taped a photo of her mother on the wall above her pillow and asked her mother to hold her each night while she slept. As she lay in bed, she could feel her mother caressing her, and her defenses softening. She described her mother's love as being like a current of energy that gave her strength. Within weeks, she could feel more ease in her body upon waking. Within months, she could feel her mother's support with her as a physical feeling throughout the day. By the end of the year, she noticed more people entering her life in a substantial way. (Note: This particular woman's mother was still alive; however, this practice is effective regardless of whether one's parent is alive or deceased.)

Consider doing this practice for ten days. Come back and write your observations here.

....
....
....

- **Developing a Supportive Image:** A sudden onset of anxiety in a seven-year-old boy expressed in his pulling out much of the hair on the crown of his head, a condition known as trichotillomania. His anxiety appeared to originate in the family history. When his mother was seven, she witnessed her mother die suddenly of a brain aneurysm. The grief was so great that his mother never talked about his grandmother. When his mother shared what had happened with him, the boy immediately began to relax. She had him imagine his deceased grandmother as a guardian angel protecting them both. She showed him a picture of a halo and had him imagine that Grandmother's love was like a halo caressing his head. Whenever he touched the top of his head, he would be met with a peaceful feeling. That day he stopped pulling his hair out.

Does this practice conjure up an image that's helpful for you? If so, in what way?

....

....

....

▶ **Creating a Boundary:** Another woman grew up burdened by feeling responsible for her alcoholic mother's happiness and well-being. As this pattern of caretaking continued into adulthood, she had difficulty letting herself receive care and support from others. It was hard for her to be in relationships without feeling both responsible for people's feelings and suffocated by their needs. In her daily practice, she sat on the floor and traced a circle around her body using a piece of yarn, noticing that, as she marked out a space for herself, she was already breathing more easily. In an inner conversation, she told her mother: "Mom, this is my space. You are over there and I am over here. When I was little, I would have done anything to make you happy, but it was way too much for me. Now I feel like I have to make everyone happy and it makes closeness feel suffocating. Mom, from now on, your feelings are over there with you and my feelings are over here with me. In this boundary, I'll honor my own feelings so that I don't have to lose myself when I start to feel connected with someone."

Draw a boundary on the floor around your body with a piece of yarn, rope, or a bathrobe sash. Visualize your mother or father outside this boundary, and write your observations here.

....
....
....

Which of the above healing experiences resonated with you the most?

....
....
....

If you were to create your own healing practice or image, what would it be?

....

....

....

The rituals and practices above may seem small in comparison to the great pain we may have carried for years, yet the more we repeat and revisit these new images and experiences, the more they integrate inside us. Science tells us that practices such as these can alter our brains by creating new neural pathways. Not only that, when we visualize a healing image, we activate the same regions of the brain—specifically in the left prefrontal cortex—that are associated with feelings of well-being and positive emotion.[4]

It's important that we practice being with our new feelings and sensations so that they can become ingrained in us. The more we practice, the more we deepen the learning. In this way, our brains can change, and we can feel more alive inside.

As you continue to do these practices, you'll likely notice a new internal experience begin to take root. It may come to you in the form of a feeling, perhaps as a sense of belonging or connection. Maybe you'll feel the support of family members watching over you. Maybe you'll experience a greater sense of peace, as if something unresolved is finally completing.

HEALING AND THE BODY

An essential part of healing involves our ability to incorporate the experience of our physical sensations into the process. When we can just "be with" the feelings that arise in our bodies without reacting unconsciously, we are more likely to stay grounded when inner unrest begins to surge. Insight is often gained when we are willing to tolerate what's uncomfortable in the quest to understand ourselves.

When you focus inside, what do you feel? What sensations do you connect with your fearful thoughts or uncomfortable emotions? Where do you feel it the most? Does your throat constrict? Does your breathing stop? Does your chest tighten? Do you go numb? Where is the epicenter of that feeling in your body? In your heart? In your belly or solar plexus? Being able to navigate this inner territory, even when the feelings seem overpowering, is essential.

Exercise: Experiencing Your Physical Sensations

If you're not sure what your body's feeling, say your core sentence aloud. As you learned in chapter 6, speaking your core sentence aloud can arouse physical sensations. Say it and observe your body. Are you aware of any shakiness? Is there a sinking feeling? Numbness? Whatever you feel or don't feel is fine. Just place your hand where you imagine or sense the feelings to be.

Next, bring your breath to that area. Exhale into your body so that the entire area feels supported. You might want to visualize your exhale as a beam of light illuminating that part of your body.

Now say to yourself: "I've got you." At the same time, send another exhale out to every cell in your body. Say the words again: "I've got you."

Imagine that you are speaking to a young child who feels unseen and unheard. Chances are there *is* a child there—a child part of you that has been ignored for a very long time. Imagine that this small child has been waiting for you to recognize him or her, and today is that day.

Now tune in to that child. What does he or she want you to know? Does he or she feel safe, or unsafe? Understood, or misunderstood? Can he or she hear your words? Can he or she feel your touch and receive your comfort? Can you feel that part of your body settling when you say the words "I've got you"? If not, say the words again and again until that young part of you can soften and trust your care.

Beyond saying the words, we need to practice being with the uncomfortable feelings in our body until we can reach what's beneath them—the sensations we experience as life-giving, sensations such as pulsing, tingling, softening, expanding, blood flowing, waves of energy, light, or warmth radiating. And then we need to be able to hold those sensations for at least a minute, and do this six times a day. That can be enough to change our brain and calm our stress response.

It's been shown that practicing mindfulness like this can actually shrink the amygdala (which often enlarges from trauma) and thicken the prefrontal cortex, that part of the brain that helps us regulate emotions and relax into inner sensations.

At the risk of sounding repetitive, I'll say it again: let the sensations of positive experiences affect you physically, viscerally, to the point where you come to know them and trust the feeling of them in your body.

What's most important is that our brains need to know we're safe, that there's no impending threat. When we're able to rest in these positive sensations, we're signaling to our amygdala: *I've got this. You don't need to send out the old alarm signals to the alarm towers of our body. You can relax now.*

One of my clients with chronic pain said the following words when he practiced being with his physical sensations: "I'll hold you gently, so you don't have to hold our body so tightly."

DISCOVERING YOUR HEALING PATHWAY

In the two chapters that follow, you'll find the same practices I use with clients, based on the four unconscious themes we explored in chapter 3. These practices contain a specific combination of healing sentences and healing images that can calm a restless body and soothe an anxious mind.

CHAPTER 9

RECONNECTING WITH OURSELVES

Healing the Break in the Bond

Not all core language stems from previous generations. There's a particular quality of core language that reflects the overwhelming experience of children who've been separated from their mothers, either physically or emotionally, causing a break in the attachment. When we've experienced a break in the bond with our mother, our words can reflect an intense anxiety that remains unseen and unhealed. We may also hear words of longing for connection as well as words of frustration, rage, judgment, criticism, or cynicism.

> ## Examples of Core Sentences from a Break in the Bond
>
> "I'll be left... I'll be abandoned... I'll be rejected... I'll be all alone... I'll die alone... I'll have nobody... I'll be helpless... I'll lose control... I don't matter... They don't want me... I'm not enough... I'm too much... They'll leave me... They'll hurt me... They'll betray me... I'll be annihilated... I'll be destroyed... I won't exist... It's hopeless."

Core sentences like these can also come from a prior generation in the family history, not necessarily from a break in the bond with our mother. We can be born into these feelings and never know where they originate. As we learned earlier, this language can be inherited from our parent's or grandparent's break in the bond with their mother.

A common theme that characterizes a break in the bond is a strong rejection of our mother, combined with a feeling of blame that she couldn't attend to our needs. This is not always the case, however. We can feel a great love for our mother but, because the bond never fully developed, feel that she was weak and fragile and that we needed to take care of her. In our need to feel bonded with her, the direction of tending can go in reverse. Unknowingly, we can attempt to provide our mother with the very nurturance we desperately need ourselves.

When we have a break in the bond, it's common to

hear core complaints and core descriptors like the ones we discussed in chapter 5. (To refresh your memory, go to page 98.)

If you believe you've experienced (or inherited) a break in the bond, I recommend addressing this trauma before you work with the other three unconscious themes. Healing your relationship with your mother will strengthen your inner experience of yourself and provide you with more feelings of well-being, as well as with the scaffolding needed to more effectively process the other work you do.

If you have a sense that your mother provided what you needed, but you still feel elements of a break in the bond expressing in your thoughts, feelings, behaviors, or relationships, you may have inherited the effects of a break in the bond from your mother or father's experience with their own mothers. In either case, the practices below can soften a hardness or release a tightness you didn't even know was there.

 **PRACTICE**

VALIDATION SENTENCES
WE'VE LONGED TO HEAR

Place a chair in the room in which you're going to sit. Then set a pair of shoes in front of you—shoes that are easy to slip on and off, like slippers or flip-flops—to represent where your mother would be standing while you're sitting in the chair. Place her shoes on the floor wherever your body signals to you that the distance feels right, somewhere between three to twelve steps away. Wherever you're guided to place the shoes is perfect.

Visualize your mother receiving the same understanding you received as you read about the effects of a break in the bond and how that can create trauma in a child.

Now read each of the sentences below, and find one or two—or more—that reflect what happened between you and your mother when you were small. Imagine your mother is speaking these sentences to you out loud. Perhaps these are sentences you've always longed to hear. Read the sentences again, either silently or aloud, and let your body receive the energy they generate.

Sentences a Mother Could Say to Her Child

1. "It's true. With all that was going on, my attention got pulled away from you when you most needed it."

2. "You needed me, but all the stress (the fighting . . . the drinking . . . the divorce . . . my sadness . . .) affected what I could give you."

3. "I called you 'my independent child,' and that wasn't the truth. You were just craving my love."

4. "If I knew then what I know now, I would have held you in my arms and told you, 'You're safe,' and 'I'm with you,' and 'There's

nothing you need to do but breathe and take in my love.'"

5. "If I had gotten more from my mother, I would have given you more."

6. "I couldn't connect deeply with you, and that must have been so painful."

7. "You were so little. It's impossible for you to remember. Let me tell you all the things that happened that made you stop trusting my love."

8. "It's true. When I was pregnant with you, I thought I'd lose you, and that massive fear flooded our bodies and disconnected us."

9. "I couldn't show you this love then, but I can show it to you now."

10. "I may not be able to show you this love in real life, but I can give it to you now."

11. "If you visualize looking in my eyes and just breathe, we can heal this."

12. "I've got you, and I'll breathe with you until you feel seen, until you feel safe, until you trust me to take care of you."

If you find yourself feeling blocked or defended while reading these sentences, keep saying them again (and even again) until a new energy begins to stir inside your body.

How does hearing these sentences feel in your body? What specifically—what sensations—do you notice?

....
....
....

Which sentence had the biggest impact?

....

Do you have an impulse to move the shoes either closer or farther away? If so, physically do so and notice what that feels like.

....
....
....

PRACTICE

HEALING THE BREAK IN THE BOND WITH A PHOTOGRAPH

The following practice can also help you repair an attachment wound with your mother without needing to be together in person. This practice is done with her photo, and it can help you dissolve the glass wall that may exist between you. It's also a way to visualize receiving her love, even if she wasn't very loving. Many of us, when there's been a break in the bond with our mother, recoil at the thought of getting close to her. This practice can help chip away at the resistance we still feel in our body.

I've given this tool to thousands of people over the last thirty years and the results have been extraordinary. Countless people have reported how, as their inner relationship with their mother began to thaw, their hard feelings softened and their outer relationship mended.

For this practice, you're going to place a photo of your mother by your bed over your left shoulder, as the left side represents feminine energy. You could either tape the photo above your pillow, or set it on the nightstand close to your left shoulder.

If you have a photo of your mother when she's younger, that would be preferable, but any photo of her will work.

At night, before you fall asleep, take a moment to gaze at the photo. Imagine that you're connecting with your mother's higher self. If that idea doesn't work for you, visualize that this practice is being guided by a higher force of some sort.

Say one or all of these sentences to her silently inside: "Mom, please hold me while I'm sleeping . . ."

- ". . . so we can heal the bond that broke between us."

- ". . . so I can learn to feel safe in my body."

- ". . . so I can feel more connected to you."

"Teach me how to trust your love, how to receive it, and how to let it in."

If you were an emotional caretaker for your mother, add this phrase:

- ". . . without having to take care of you, Mom. Just receiving."

Now visualize a current or flow of energy coming from the photo, entering you as a sensory download. Feel the sensations enter your body. Visualize these sensations as a calm, loving energy soothing you. Imagine you're soaking in this energy. Feel it going into your cells. Notice if the energy is more like particles or waves. Does it have a color, temperature, or texture? However you feel it is fine.

As you take this energy in, feel your body softening, opening. Let it soak into you like mist, or rain, or light. Whatever image comes to you is the right image. If no image comes, let yourself feel it's happening anyway. Keep the practice going until you feel drenched in this energy.

Do this for at least sixty seconds. Feel the energy of this connection, of being held, of being calmed, of being loved—even if it didn't happen when you were small. Your brain doesn't care if it happened in real life or not. It just wants the healing and will experience it as real. If this practices resonates with you, do it for 90 days.

When you do this practice, what do you notice physically? If you feel peaceful or relaxed, how does your body indicate that? What are the sensations?

....

....

....

 **PRACTICE**

HEALING SENTENCES THAT RECONNECT US WITH OURSELVES

When we've had a break in the bond with our mother, we often don't know what to do with the uncomfortable feelings in our body. In the following practice, we'll learn how to just be with them. We'll learn how to integrate the sensations until we're able to enter an embodied experience of ease. Let's do that now.

First, observe what feels unsettling in your body. Maybe you feel tightness, numbness, nausea, anxiety, or some other form of distress. Maybe you're aware of a hollow or empty feeling inside, a part of you that feels blocked, or disappeared, or disconnected.

Whatever you feel, place your hands there. Often, these sensations live in the throat, chest, solar plexus, belly, or womb.

Now breathe into that part of your body and visualize your breath as a gentle wind, calming a small child—a young child part of you that craves your attention. Maybe that child feels all alone, like there's no one there. Maybe he or she feels vulnerable and frightened, or armored and guarded, and says, *I don't need anybody.*

Hold that child in your breath and say one or more of these healing sentences:

"I've got you."

"I'm here."

"I'll hold you until you feel seen."

"I'll breathe with you until you feel safe."

"I won't leave you."

"I'll breathe with you until you trust me to take care of you."

When we place our hands on our body and direct our words and breath inside, we support the young part of us that feels most vulnerable. In doing so, we have a chance to ease or release sensations we experience as intolerable. Long-standing feelings of discomfort can finally give way to feelings of expansion and well-being.

With your hands on your body, keep repeating the sentences above and expand that well-being now. Keep breathing until you can feel positive, energetic sensations in the core of your body—warmth, tingling, the pulsing of your blood, waves of energy, a current flowing up and down, back and forth, in and out, spiraling round and round, in the shape of a figure eight, however it shows up. Now visualize any uncomfortable feelings dissolving into this energy.

What did you first notice in your body that felt unsettling? On the body map below, mark the area with the sensation you experienced.

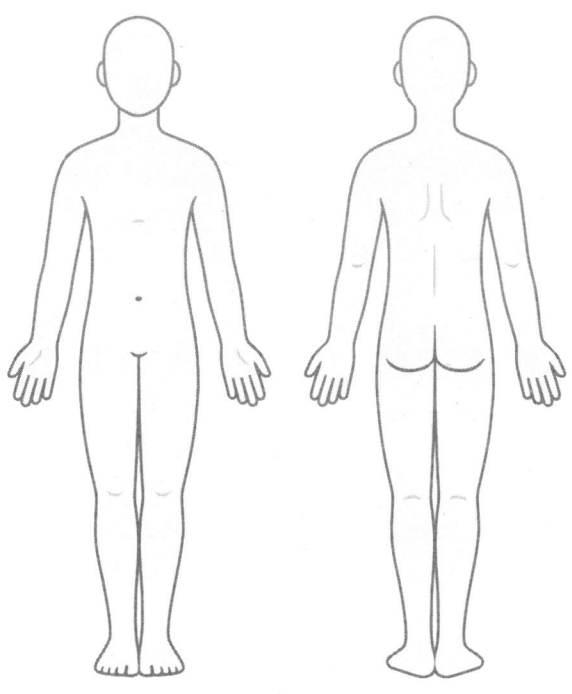

Did your energy change as you placed your hands there and said those sentences? If so, how? Write about your experience.

....

....

....

Remember, new sensations and new feelings are how we feed our prefrontal cortex so our brains can change and our stress responses can quiet.

> **Because Susan** often felt disconnected from her own body, I suggested she do the above practice and say the healing sentences to reconnect with herself. What felt most unsettling to Susan was a tight, aching feeling in her heart area and a raw, nauseous feeling in her lower belly, so she placed one hand on her heart and another at her womb.
>
> With her hands on her body, she breathed deeply and slowly, as if she were calming a small child—the young part of her who felt she needed to handle everything on her own.
>
> As she repeated the sentences "I've got you" and "I'll breathe with you until you trust me to take care of you," she began to sense her own energy expanding from within, and her body began to gently rock, as though it were moving in the shape of a figure eight.
>
> Susan continued this practice, holding the sensation of rocking for one minute, and did this six times a day. Within weeks, not only had the ache in her heart subsided, but the frozen shoulder she'd been grappling with for months began to release. Susan reported that she was now able to ask the people closest to her for help and was able to receive it.

CHAPTER 10

RECONNECTING WITH OTHERS

Healing Generational Trauma

Now that you've practiced the exercises above, you're ready for the next step—bringing your awareness to the other three unconscious themes.

- ▶ Merging with a parent
- ▶ Rejecting a parent
- ▶ Identifying with a family member other than a parent

HEALING PRACTICES FOR MERGING WITH A PARENT

When we merge with a parent, we unconsciously share or repeat that parent's feelings, behaviors, experiences, or misfortunes. In chapter 3, we explored the four dynamics of merging. I'll repeat them here:

- ▶ **I'll follow you.** A child might try to die early to join his or her deceased parent in death, by taking drugs, driving recklessly, practicing extreme sports, or engaging in other high-risk behaviors.

- ▶ **I'll share it with you.** A child might try to join a parent in his or her misfortune: the parent may have been treated poorly in his or her relationship, lost their great love, drank too much, failed financially, lived in poor health, et cetera, and the child repeats the behavior.

- ▶ **I'll do it in your place.** A child might take on emotions the parent couldn't process: "If you can't feel the grief of what happened to you, I'll feel all of it." Or, "If you're unhappy and want to die, I'll become depressed, anorexic, or suicidal."

- ▶ **I'll atone for you.** A child unconsciously pays for something that happened in the past: "I'll go to jail, or take my life, or become sick to atone for what you did."

Merging with a parent can cloud our identity and drain our individuality. By reliving experiences that didn't originate with us, we can lose the gravity of who we are. The following practices can help us regain our sense of sovereignty and inner power. If you don't feel safe doing them alone, consider working with a therapist so you have the support you need.

PRACTICE

HEALING SENTENCES TO BREAK A MERGED RELATIONSHIP

If you've merged with your mother or father, place a pair of slip-on shoes on the floor in front of you, where you envision that parent (or both parents) to be standing. Now read the following sentences as though you're hearing them said by your parent(s). Imagine your parent's voice saying these words as your body opens to receive them. Note which sentences reach you in the deepest way.

Sentences Your Parent Could Say to You

1. "I love you for who you are. There's nothing you have to do to earn my love."

2. "You are my child, and you're separate from me. My feelings do not have to be your feelings."

3. "I've been too close to you, and I see the toll it has taken on you."

4. "It must have been overwhelming with all my needs and emotions."

5. "My needs made it difficult for you to have space for yourself."

6. "I will step back now so that my love doesn't overpower you."

7. "I will give you all the space you need."

8. "I have been too close to you for you to know yourself. Now I will stay over here and take joy in watching you live your life over there."

9. "You have been taking care of me and I have allowed it—but no more."

10. "This is way too much for any child."

11. "Any child who tried to fix this would feel burdened."

12. "This is not yours."

13. "Take a step back now until you can feel your own life flowing through you. Only then will I be at peace."

14. "I have not been able to face my own pain until now. What's mine has been over there with you. It's time for it to return to me, where it belongs. Then we're both free."

15. "You have had far too much of me and not enough of your mother/father. It would please me to see the two of you closer. That's where you need to be."

Now, as you visualize your parent standing in front of you, notice if *you* have an inner feeling to move forward or backward. Do you need to move closer or farther away? Do you have a body feeling that lets you know what distance is right for you? The right distance can open, soften, or relax something inside of us. When this happens, we have more room inside to feel our feelings.

When you've found your right distance, say one or more of the following sentences to your parent. Notice your feelings as the words are spoken.

Sentences You Could Say to Your Parent

1. "Mom/Dad, I'm over here, and you're over there."

2. "Your feelings are over there with you, and my feelings are over here with me."

3. "Please stay over there, but don't go too far away."

4. "I breathe much easier when I have my own space."
5. "It shrinks me when I try to take care of your feelings."
6. "It was too much to think I could make you happy."
7. "I see now that setting myself aside has only made us both invisible."
8. "You had your turn. Now, it's my turn. I promise to honor you by living my life fully."
9. "From now on, I'll live my life fully, knowing that you are there behind me, supporting me."
10. "Thank you for seeing me and hearing me."

As you say these sentences, do you notice any new emotions or feelings surfacing? How would you describe it?

....

....

....

Can you feel yourself (or your parents) being touched as the words are received?

....

....

....

PRACTICE

TAKING YOUR OWN SPACE

The following exercise can deepen your visceral awareness—the felt sense inside your body—of how a merged relationship with a parent may have affected you, and can help you break free.

Find two pairs of slip-on shoes, one pair to represent you, and the other to represent the parent you merged with.

Place both pairs on the floor, arranging them however feels right. Maybe one pair is turned toward the other, while the other is facing away. Maybe both pairs are turned toward each other, or both pairs are turned away. Maybe they're far apart, or very, very close—almost on top of each other. With your parent's "footprints" on the floor, you're bringing to life a dynamic that existed when you were young.

Stand in the pair of shoes that represent you. How does it feel to stand here with this parent? What physical sensations do you notice? What emotions are you aware of? Take a few minutes to let the feelings arise.

Now stand in your parent's shoes. What might he or she be feeling standing there with you? Lonely? Sad? Fragile? Disconnected? Stressed? Needing to receive something from you? Take a moment to feel that.

You might even put another pair of shoes on the floor to represent your other parent. What happens when the second parent is brought in? Does the first parent feel better or worse?

Now, move *your* footprints to a place in the room where your energy isn't entangled with either parent—where you feel free, where nothing is being asked of you, where you feel the strength of your own sovereign energy.

To feel even freer, you might want to get a piece of yarn and lay it front of your footprints, creating a boundary to give you even more space.

Now stand in your footprints and feel what it's like to have a boundary. Note any new feelings and sensations.

Consider saying these words: "Mom/Dad, this is my boundary. This is my space. Only I get to be in here. Your energy has to stay over there with you. It stays outside of my boundary."

You might even get another piece of yarn and lay it in front of your parent's footprints to keep their energy inside their boundary.

Now say these words: "Mom/Dad, you're over there, and I'm over here. Your feelings are over there with you, and my feelings are over here with me."

Standing in your footprints, feel the new sensations that having a boundary and saying these words create. Let yourself be surprised at what emerges.

Write down the emotions, feelings, and sensations you felt while standing as your parent.

....

....

....

Now write down the emotions, feelings, and sensations you felt while standing as you—in your own sovereign energy.

....
....
....

PRACTICE

HEALING SENTENCES FOR THE FOUR DYNAMICS OF MERGING

Below are examples of the types of healing sentences we can say to free ourselves when we're caught in the web of merging.

Dynamic 1: I'll Follow You

Example: "Dad, I've been taking terrible risks: riding my motorcycle without a helmet, driving too fast, taking dangerous jumps. I now realize I've been unconsciously trying to join you by dying early like you did. I know this isn't what you want for me, and it's definitely not what I want. My death would serve no purpose, and it would only make everyone feel worse. From now on, I'll honor you by valuing the life you gave me, so that I can leave a legacy of a life lived well, and not a life cut short."

Dynamic 2: I'll Share It with You

Example 1: "Mom, you and Dad had your turn, and I know it didn't go well. And I can't do anything about that. But it's my turn now, and I plan to make the most of it. I'll honor you and Dad by having a good relationship with my partner, because I know that's what you both ultimately want for me."

Example 2: "Mom, you blamed yourself when you found Lucy dead in her crib. Your pain was like a cloud blanketing the whole family. For years, I've felt panic when terrible things happen that I can't control. I blame myself and don't want to live. Now I can see that these feelings didn't start with me. They were yours. They were part of your growth and your strength—and I can't take that away from you. By sharing your pain, I thought I could save you. But all I did was take on feelings that weren't mine. Now, when I feel this panic in my chest, I'll breathe it back to you—back where it belongs."

Dynamic 3: I'll Do It in Your Place

Example: "Dad, ever since you came back from the war, things haven't been right. You've been depressed and refuse to talk about what happened there. Because so many died, maybe you feel guilty being alive. And I've been acting out those feelings by drinking too much, taking drugs, and putting my life in danger, when I realize it's not me who wants to die. I've been feeling what you can't let yourself feel, and it's only going to lead to more tragedy. As of today, I choose life. I will live fully, and leave your feelings with you, embodying only those that are mine."

Dynamic 4: I'll Atone for You

Example: "Mom, I've been struggling with this health condition for nearly twenty years. It started at exactly the same age you were when you hit that boy on his bicycle. Your life changed after that. And I need to change mine too. I can't keep paying the price for what you did. To honor you and to honor that boy, I'll take my life seriously and make the health changes I need to live fully."

After reading these examples, is there a way in which you've been sharing or reliving your parents' pain? How so?

....
....
....

What healing sentence(s) would free you from this dynamic?

....
....
....

HEALING PRACTICES WHEN WE'VE REJECTED A PARENT

As you may remember from chapter 3, when we reject a parent, it can operate unconsciously in three different ways:

- **We reject a part of ourselves.** The behaviors we dislike in our parents get disowned in us, and then can express unconsciously.

- **Our unhealed relationship with our parent gets projected onto others.** We'll either pull in partners with similar traits who treat us in the same way, or we'll do the opposite; we'll attract kind partners, yet see them as uncaring.

- **We'll do to ourselves the very thing we believe was done to us.** If our parent was critical or aggressive, we can become self-critical and inwardly aggressive, treating our inner child the same way.

If we truly want to embrace life and experience joy, if we truly want deep and satisfying relationships, if we truly want to live up to our full potential, we must first repair our broken relationships with our parents. Beyond having given us life and being an inexorable part of who we are, our parents are the gateway to the hidden strengths and creative forces, as well as the challenges, that are also part of our ancestral legacy. Whether they're dead or alive, whether we're distant from them or our relationship is amicable, our parents—and the traumas they've experienced or inherited—hold a significant key to our healing. Even if we can't do it in person, it's essential that we heal these relationships, at the very least, in our inner images.

If you feel you've rejected a parent, the next step is to find a way to soften the hardness you may feel in your heart toward them, as well as to own the qualities you share with them. In the heart, we have a chance to transform something difficult into something that brings strength. Qualities like cruelty can become the source of our kindness; our judgments can forge the foundation of our compassion.

When Parents Have Caused Harm

Being at peace with ourselves often begins with being at peace with our parents. That said, if our parents were extremely hurtful, or the damage between you is too great, healing can still happen in our inner images. I've had several clients who were unable to heal with their parents in person, but were able to visualize healing with their parents' higher selves, or with the part of them that would have given more if they could have. Or they imagined that the process of healing was being guided by a higher force of some sort. However we get there doesn't matter—the brain wants healing and will embrace our inner images as though they are real-life events.

Reconciliation is mostly an internal movement. It's an inside job. Our relationship with our parents is not dependent on what

they do, how they are, or how they respond. It's about what we do. The change occurs in us.

Until we heal those relationships, we can unconsciously project onto others, and onto seemingly random situations, what remains unfinished with the parents we had when we were small. Healing can happen even if they've passed on, sit in jail, or tread in a sea of pain. Is there one memory, one good intention, one tender image, one way your parents expressed love, that you can let in? Letting yourself connect with a warm inner image can begin to change your outer relationship with your parents. You can't change what was, but you can change what is, as long as you don't expect your parents to be any different from who they are. It is you who must hold the relationship differently. That's your work. Not your parents' work. The question is: Are you willing to do it?

> **Before you** attempt to heal a severely broken relationship with your parents in person, you might first want to have a few sessions with a body-centered therapist or cultivate a mindfulness meditation practice to learn resources that will allow you to connect with your body's sensations. When you can observe your reactions to another's emotions, you can monitor and give yourself what you need in the very moments you most need it. It's important to cultivate an inner feeling that both guides and supports you.

For example, certain breathing techniques can give you a physical sense of your body's limits so that you can proceed at a speed that's just right for you, as well as maintain the distance you feel is appropriate. The right distance allows you to feel relaxed, so that you don't have to defend or shrink yourself to feel connected. A solid but flexible boundary enables you to have adequate space to feel your feelings while, at the same time, letting you enjoy the healing connection you're forging with your parents. Ultimately, when you can breathe deeply enough to know what you're feeling in your body, you don't have to leave it.

It's only after we've done a significant amount of inner work—to understand how to navigate our emotions, learn how to feel safe in our body, and develop clear but flexible boundaries—that we can attempt reconciliation in real time with hurtful parents.

Do you have any positive memories being with your parents? Can you stay open in your body when you think about them? If they're still alive, can you remain undefended when you're with them? Write down your observations.

....

....

....

If you still can't imagine reaching out to your parent, even in your inner image, it may help to ask: What traumas happened to them, or in their family history, that blocked their love from flowing? What traumas made them behave in a certain way? What sits behind their distance, criticism, or aggression?

Questions such as these take things out of the realm of what's personal. Instead, we begin to understand that any parent who experienced this type of trauma (or inherited it from their parents) may not have much love to give and could even be hurtful or volatile with their children. Simply put, traumatic events may have blocked the flow of love and closed their hearts. It doesn't excuse what they did, but it can help to explain. That understanding alone can free us to heal those relationships, inwardly or outwardly, and can help us calm the brain's stress response that keeps us locked in a state of suffering.

So if you still find yourself shrinking or feeling defensive, or you go into caretaking mode, there's probably more inner work that needs to be done before you attempt to heal the relationship in person. Let's begin that inner work now, by revisiting the trails of trauma in your family history that may have affected your parents and what they were able to give.

# PRACTICE

THE FLOW OF LOVE

Now we're going to look at your mother's and father's family trees. The genograms below represent three generations that include your parents, their parents, and their parents' parents.

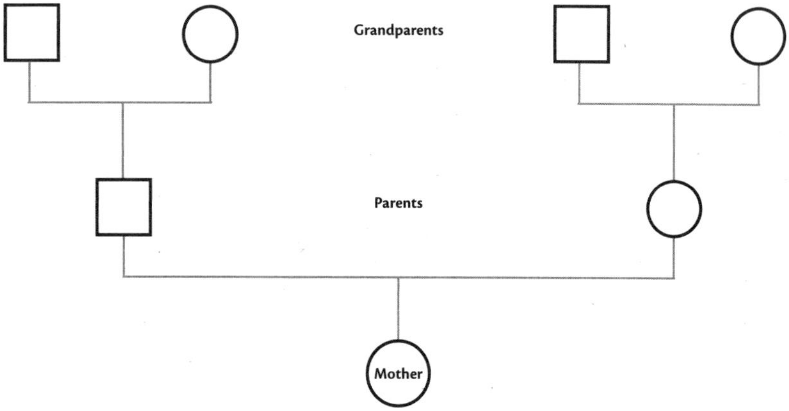

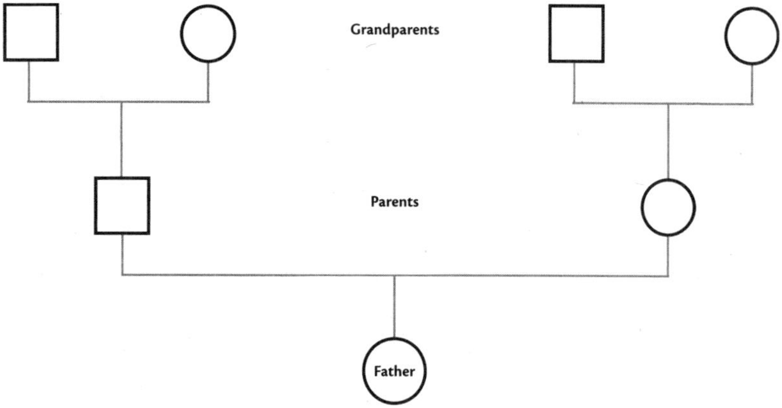

Next to each square or circle, in all three generations, write down the traumatic events or experiences that may have blocked the flow of love to *your* parents, especially the events that occurred when your parents were young.

Next, write down the emotional qualities that describe your grandparents. How would your mother and father describe the love they received from them? Were your grandparents warm, openhearted, loving? Or were they unloving? Did either of your parents experience a break in the bond with their mother? If so, was it due to a physical separation, an emotional separation, or an experience that occurred in the womb? Write down what you know.

As well, write down any other stories you know. Was someone violent, or having affairs, or an alcoholic? Stressful experiences like these often break the bond a mother's forming with her child.

Now look at the genograms you created. What does it show you about the love your parents received, and the love they were able to give?

....

....

....

Look back another generation. What kind of parenting did your grandparents receive?

....
....
....

List the traumatic events and experiences that blocked the flow of love to your parents.

....
....
....

Seeing what your parents may have gone through, are you able to feel more compassion for them?

....
....
....

PRACTICE

THREE MAGIC SENTENCES

If you feel ready to heal with your parents in real time, here are three of my favorite healing sentences you could say to your parent that have the power to transform the relationship. These sentences work on an energetic level to soften the hard edges of memories that keep the story going, the story that keeps you and your parent disconnected.

1. "Mom/Dad, I really like that we're close."

2. "You're a good mother/father." Then share a memory about how that's true. (For example, "Dad, when I was six and broke my ankle, you held my hand all the way to the emergency room.")

3. "I'm sorry for how distant I've been. From now on, I promise to be more connected." Even if you're not sure you can keep this promise, consider saying the words anyway, and then notice the effect they have in your body.

Feel the energy of these sentences. How do you imagine your parent would feel hearing these words from you? How might they respond? Would one or two of these sentences be possible to slip into a conversation?

Take the first one, for example: "I really like that we're close." Hearing this sentence, your parent might think: *What? He thinks we're close! I didn't know that. That's wonderful!* Such a sentence works energetically and gives each of you more permission to take the risks that can actually forge a closer bond. Sometimes just saying a sentence like this can open something inside us that surprises us.

 **PRACTICE**

ADDITIONAL HEALING SENTENCES TO SAY TO A PARENT

Read the list of healing sentences that follows. Some of them are similar to the three magic sentences. Perhaps one or two of them will speak to you in a way that starts to dissolve the block between you and your parents. Let the words touch you. Is there a sentence that tugs at your heart? Perhaps you can imagine saying one or two of these sentences in person to the parent you have rejected.

If you're doing this practice in your inner images, you could place a pair of shoes on the floor in front of you to represent that parent. Or use their photo. Is it easier to say these sentences to the shoes or photo? It doesn't matter which version of the practice you choose. The essential piece is saying the sentences and letting them reach you.

Remember, positive experiences and practices that make us feel good in our body are how we heal. When we grow the good feelings, our brain can change. This is true even if we have to "fake it till we make it" at first.

Healing Sentences When We Have Rejected a Parent

1. "I'm so sorry for how distant I've been."

2. "From now on, I promise to be closer."

3. "Whenever you reached out to me, I pushed you away."
4. "I miss you, but it's not easy to tell you that."
5. "I closed my heart so it wouldn't hurt so much, but now I want to open it and let you in."
6. "I've been so judgmental, it prevented me from being close to you."
7. "I'd really like to be closer."
8. "I like that we're close."
9. "You're a really good father/mother." (Share an example with him/her.)
10. "I promise to stop making you prove your love to me."
11. "I'll stop expecting that your love should look a certain way."
12. "I promise to take in your love as you give it—not as I expect it."
13. "I'll take in your love even when I can't feel it in your words."
14. "You've given me a lot and I promise to do something good with it."
15. "Mom/Dad, can we just sit here together? It feels good just sitting here."

How does it feel to say these sentences? Can you feel something opening inside you when you say them? Can you visualize your parent receiving them?

....
....
....

If you said these sentences to your parent's shoes or photo, do you have a sense of your parent receiving them?

....
....
....

Do you have a sense of an energetic field that links you together?

....
....
....

Write down your experiences here.

....
....
....
....

....
....
....
....
....
....

PRACTICE

HEALING SENTENCES TO SAY TO A DECEASED PARENT

Even when our parents are deceased, we can still speak to them. I find speaking directly to their photo can create an energy that may surprise you. Here are a few sentences that can help rebuild a bond that broke or never fully developed:

1. "Please hold me in my sleep when my body is more open and I'm easier to reach."
2. "Please teach me how to trust your love, how to receive it, and how to let it in."
3. "Please help me feel more peace in my body."

PRACTICE

HEALING SENTENCES TO SAY TO AN UNKNOWN OR ESTRANGED PARENT

When a parent has left early or has given us away to be raised by others, the pain can feel insurmountable, and the terror of being left can forge an unconscious blueprint for the many rejections and abandonments that occur later in our life. The cycle of pain needs to come to an end. As long as we continue to live feeling that we've been wronged or victimized, we're likely to continue the pattern. Read the following sentences and imagine that you are saying them to your estranged parent or to the parent you never met.

1. "If it made things easier for you to leave or give me away, I understand."

2. "I'll stop blaming you, which I know only holds us both hostage."

3. "I'll get what I need from others and make something good come out of what happened."

4. "What happened between us will serve as the source of my strength."

5. "Because this happened, I've gained a particular strength I can rely on."

6. "Thank you for the gift of life. I promise not to waste or squander it."

PRACTICE

INITIATING CONTACT WITH AN ESTRANGED PARENT

Even when our outer relationship with our parents is distant or nonexistent, our inner relationship with them continues to evolve. If you and your parent are out of touch—maybe one of you refuses to speak to the other, or you can't calm your body when you're with them—it's still possible to begin the healing process. You might consider sending them a text, email, or letter just to let them know you're okay. Maybe on a birthday or a holiday, you could text, "Hi, Mom. I just wanted you to know I'm doing okay. I didn't want you to worry." Or, "Hi, Dad. I just want you to know things are going well. The kids are doing great—they're playing Little League this year." You'll know if making contact feels right. Trust your body. Feel whether you get a green light or a red light. Your body always knows.

What I might say to my parent:

....

....

....

HEALING AN IDENTIFICATION WITH A FAMILY MEMBER (OTHER THAN A PARENT)

Maybe you've come to this point in the workbook and you've done all the suggested practices, but you still feel something unfinished. Look back at your core complaint, core sentence, and core trauma. Could it be that you are entangled with a family member from the past? Could it be your grandmother, grandfather, uncle, aunt, or older half sibling? Or could this person not even be related to you, but may have caused or experienced some type of suffering connected with someone in your family?

If you feel caught up in this type of dynamic, trapped in thoughts or feelings that don't belong to you, try the practice below to break the entanglement.

 **PRACTICE**

BREAKING AN UNCONSCIOUS IDENTIFICATION

Place a pair of slip-on shoes on the floor to represent the footprints of the person you're entangled with. Allow the shoes to guide you where to put them and which direction they face. Now step back and feel this person standing there. Imagine what it must have been like when this person experienced unhappiness or suffering.

Now step into their footprints and let your mind go blank. Stand there, without any preconceived ideas, and let this person's feelings appear in your body. Experience their emotions and sensations, as well as any impulses that show up in your body. Does your body want to lean forward, fall backward, crumple to the ground, or something else?

It can be intense to feel the emotions of a person you're identified with, so only do this practice if you feel safe and have support to process it.

Visualize that this person has come into the room to help you break an entanglement that has been tying up your life force energy for far too long. You were merely following an unconscious stream of energy that was flowing from your family history.

Acknowledge that this person's feelings don't belong to you. Say it out loud. Tell them that these feelings aren't yours. For example, tell your grandmother, "This sadness isn't mine." Or tell your aunt, "This feeling of going crazy, Aunt Elma, isn't mine." Or "This impulse in my body that I could harm someone doesn't belong to me, Grandpa." Or "This feeling that I could be harmed, or stolen from, Uncle Andrew, was never mine."

Now, locate the physical feelings that don't belong to you. Place your hand on the sensations where you feel them in your body and breathe in. Then exhale these feelings back to the person you've been entangled with. Keep inhaling and exhaling until all the feelings dissolve. Feel this person welcoming these feelings back, telling you, "Breathe these feelings back to me, all of them. They were never yours. They're mine, and they belong to me."

How does it feel to do this practice? What changes or releases in your body?

....

....

....

Additional Language to Break an Unconscious Entanglement

Here are some examples of practices and sentences we can use to free ourselves from an unconscious identification.

Example 1: You've been entangled with a grandmother who felt responsible for her child's death. Place a photo of your grandmother in your living room, bedroom, meditation space, or on your desk. As you walk by the photo, imagine you can hear your grandmother say: "These feelings don't belong to you. Every time you feel as though you could harm *your* child, just breathe those feelings back to me. Feel me supporting you to keep and enjoy your child, even though I didn't get to keep mine."

Example 2: You've been entangled with ancestors who were impoverished. Maybe they lost everything in the Great Depression or had their belongings stolen or stripped away. Maybe they were sold into slavery, or were refugees of war. Whatever the case, you've been unconsciously entangled with them and have had difficulties making ends meet. Visualize these ancestors standing at your back, encouraging you to succeed. Hear them say: "From now on, we stand behind you, supporting you. You don't have to live small, or destitute, or unhappy as we did. We worked hard, hopeful that our children and grandchildren would have more than we did. That *you* would have more than we did. The best way to honor us is to embrace your life and live with the comforts you deserve."

Example 3: Your grandparent died early, creating suffering for your parent when he or she was small. Entangled with this grandparent, maybe you don't live fully or express your creativity in a way that fulfills you. Maybe you procrastinate and never bring your ideas to fruition. If so, place a photo of your grandparent in your living room, bedroom, meditation space, or on your desk. Tell this grandparent: "Grandma/Grandpa, you didn't get to live long enough to see your dreams materialize. Unconsciously connected to you, I've been squelching mine. Please stand behind me and bless me, so that I can have the strength to bring my creations to light."

After reading these three examples, do any other healing sentences come to you? What could you do or say to break the entanglement?

....

....

....

The practices in these last two chapters have been designed to free you from the effects of early or generational trauma. In doing these practices, maybe you feel a new kind of peace inside yourself. The healing sentences you've spoken (either silently or aloud) and the images, rituals, and exercises you've experienced may have helped to strengthen your connection with yourself, strengthen a relationship with a loved one, or ease an unconscious entanglement with a family member.

Now let's bring these experiences into the larger circles of your life. Let's explore how to apply what you've learned about your family history to your relationships and to your success in life and work.

CHAPTER 11

REDISCOVERING CONNECTION IN YOUR RELATIONSHIPS

The ancient poet Virgil declared, "Love conquers all." If only our love is great enough, our relationships, no matter how difficult, will surely succeed. Even the Beatles tell us, "Love is all you need." Yet, with the myriad unconscious loyalties that operate invisibly under the surface of our lives, it might be more apt to say that love—the unconscious love expressed in families—can "conquer" our ability to sustain a loving relationship with our partner.

Any unfinished business we have with one or both of our parents is often projected onto our partner. Whether we're male or female, one rule of thumb appears to hold true: *What we feel we didn't get from our mother, what remains unresolved in our relationship with her, often sets the stage for what we experience with our partner.* For example, if we experienced our mother as aloof, and felt rejected by her, we're likely to also feel rejected by our partner.

As long as we remain caught in the web of family patterns, our relationships are likely to struggle. When we learn, however, to untangle the invisible threads of family history, we can unravel their influence upon us. By making visible what has been invisible, we become freer to give and receive love.

The following questions will help you begin to decipher your core language in your intimate relationship. If you're not currently in an intimate relationship, think about your last significant relationship as if it were happening now and answer the following questions.

EXERCISE

CONNECTING YOUR CORE LANGUAGE MAP TO YOUR RELATIONSHIP

What is your greatest complaint about your partner?

What are your core descriptors of your parents—adjectives and phrases that describe them?

....

Are there any similarities between your core descriptors of your parents and your complaint about your partner?

....
....
....

What is your core sentence—your worst fear, the worst thing that could ever happen to you?

....

Write a second core sentence about being in a relationship. What is your worst fear, the worst thing that could happen to you in a relationship?

....

Does your relationship core sentence share any similarities with your original core sentence?

....
....
....

What is your core trauma—the tragic events that occurred in your childhood or family history?

....

Can you hear any echoes of your core descriptors, core sentence, or core trauma in your complaint about your partner?

....
....
....

What family member(s) may have had a similar complaint about their partner(s)?

....
....
....

Is your early relationship with your mother reflected in your relationship with your partner? If so, how?

....
....
....

20 INVISIBLE DYNAMICS THAT CAN AFFECT RELATIONSHIPS

With your core language map in mind, now consider the following family dynamics that can erode intimacy with your partner. Some of these dynamics might even keep you from entering a relationship at all. Which one or ones apply to you?

1. **You had a difficult relationship with your mother.** What's unfinished with your mother is likely to repeat with your partner.

2. **You reject, judge, or blame a parent.** The emotions, traits, and behaviors you reject in a parent are likely to live on unconsciously in you. You might project the complaints you have about that parent onto your partner. You might also attract a partner who embodies qualities similar to those of the rejected parent. When you reject a parent, you might balance this rejection by struggling in your relationships. You might leave your partners or experience being left by them. Your relationships might feel empty, or you might opt to stay alone. A close bond with the same-sexed parent appears to strengthen our capacity to commit to a partner.

3. **You are merged with the feelings of a parent.** If one parent feels negatively toward the other, it is possible that you will continue these feelings toward your partner. Feelings of discontent toward a partner can be carried intergenerationally.

4. **You experienced a break in the early bond with your mother.** With this dynamic, you likely experience some degree of anxiety when you attempt

to bond with a partner in an intimate relationship. Often the anxiety increases as the relationship deepens. Unaware that the anxiety stems from a break with your mother, you might find fault with your partner or create other conflicts that allow you to distance yourself from the closeness. You might also experience yourself as feeling needy, clingy, jealous, or insecure. Or conversely, you appear independent and don't ask for much in your relationships. Perhaps you avoid relationships altogether.

5. **You took care of a parent's feelings.** Ideally, parents give and children receive. But for many children with a sad, depressed, anxious, or insecure parent, the focus can be more about giving comfort than about receiving it. In such a dynamic, the child's experience of getting his needs met can become secondary, and the experience of having access to his gut feelings can be overshadowed by the habitual impulse to give out care rather than take it in. Later in life, this child might give too much to his partner, straining the relationship. Or the opposite can be true. Feeling overwhelmed or burdened by the needs of his partner, he can become resentful or feel emotionally blocked as the relationship evolves.

6. **Your parents were unhappy together.** If your parents struggled or didn't do well together, it's possible that you won't allow yourself to have more

than they had. An unconscious loyalty to your parents may prevent you from being any happier than they were, even if you know that happiness is what they truly want for you. In a family where exuberance is limited, children can feel guilty or uncomfortable when they are happy.

7. **Your parents didn't stay together.** If your parents didn't stay together, you might unconsciously leave your relationship as well. This can happen when you reach the same age they were when they separated, when you've spent the same amount of time in your relationship, or when your child reaches the same age that you were when your parents separated. Or you'll stay in your relationship, but live emotionally separated.

8. **Your parent or grandparent jilted a former partner.** If, for example, your father or grandfather left a former wife, or left a partner who was led to believe that the relationship would lead to marriage, you, as the daughter or granddaughter, might atone for this by remaining alone like the woman. You could feel "not good enough," like the woman who was not good enough for your father or grandfather. The same dynamic could exist for a son or grandson whose mother or grandmother left a former husband or partner.

9. **Your parent's great love broke his or her heart.** You, as the child, might unconsciously join your

parent in his or her brokenheartedness. You might lose your first love, or carry the lovelorn feelings of your parent, or feel imperfect or not good enough (as she or he did). You might feel that you are never with the partner you want. As the son, you might energetically try to replace the first love and become like a partner to your mother. As the daughter, you also might energetically try to replace the first love and become like a partner to your father.

10. **Your parent or grandparent remained alone.** If one of your parents or grandparents stayed alone after they were left or widowed, you might stay alone as well. If you are in a relationship, you might create conflict or distance so that you too feel alone. In silent allegiance, you unconsciously find a way to share their loneliness.

11. **Your parent or grandparent suffered in marriage.** If, for example, your grandmother was trapped in a loveless marriage, or your grandfather died, drank, gambled, or left, leaving your grandmother alone to raise the children, you, as the grandchild, could unconsciously associate these experiences with being married. You might either repeat her experience or resist committing to a partner for fear that the same thing could happen to you.

12. **Your parent was disparaged or disrespected by the other parent.** You, as the child, might recreate

that parent's experience by being disrespected by your partner.

13. **Your parent died young.** If a parent died in your childhood, you might physically or emotionally distance yourself from your partner when you reach the same age as the dead parent, when you've spent the same amount of time in your relationship, or when your child reaches the same age that you were when your parent died.

14. **One of your parents mistreated the other.** If one of your parents treated the other poorly, you might align with the "oppressor" parent and reenact the same dynamic with your partner. By also mistreating your partner, your parent doesn't remain "the bad one" alone. You share that role. Conversely, you could align with the "oppressed" parent and have a partner who mistreats you. Ultimately, it could be difficult for you to have more happiness than either parent who remained locked in conflict.

15. **You hurt a former partner.** If you hurt a former partner, you might unconsciously attempt to balance this hurt by sabotaging your new relationship. The new partner, unconsciously aware that he or she could receive similar treatment, might even keep a little distance from you.

16. **You've had a lot of partners.** If you've had a lot of partners, you may have eroded your ability to

bond in a relationship. Separations can become easier. Relationships can lose their depth.

17. **You had an abortion or gave a child up for adoption.** In your guilt, remorse, or regret, you might not allow yourself much happiness in a relationship.

18. **You were your mother's confidant.** As a child, you attempted to satisfy your mother's unmet needs and supply her with what she felt she couldn't get from your father. Later on, you might experience difficulty committing in a relationship. You might shut down emotionally or physically, fearing that your partner, like your mother, will want or need too much from you. A boy who was his mother's confidant often creates quick relationships with women—relationships he hasn't fully earned. He can even become a womanizer, leaving a trail of broken hearts in his wake. The remedy is a closer bond with his father.

19. **You were your father's favorite.** A girl who is closer to her father than to her mother often feels dissatisfied with the partners she selects. The root of the problem is not the partner; it's the distance she feels toward her mother. A woman's relationship with her mother can be an indicator of how fulfilling her relationship will be with her partner.

20. **Someone in the family didn't marry.** You could be identified with a parent, grandparent, aunt, uncle, or older sibling who never married. Perhaps this person was looked down upon, ridiculed, or perceived as having less than the other family members. Unconsciously aligned, you might also not marry.

Is one or more of these dynamics affecting your relationship? How?

....
....
....

Now, return to your complaint about your partner. Write it again here.

My complaint about my partner is . . .

....
....

Read your complaint out loud. Try to listen to the words without blaming your partner or losing yourself in the emotions.

Now ask yourself the following questions. For any "yes" responses, use the lines below to write down your thoughts, feelings, memories, or experiences.

Do I have the same complaint about my mother or father?

....
....
....

Did my mother or father have the same complaint about the other?

....
....
....

Did my grandmother or grandfather struggle in a similar way?

....
....

Is there a parallel between two or three generations?

....
....
....

Does my experience with my partner mirror how I felt as a small child with my mother? If so, how?

....
....
....

PRACTICE
FREEING YOUR RELATIONSHIP FROM YOUR PARENTS' ENERGY

If you've realized your parents' relationship may be influencing your current relationship, the following practice can help set you free.

Place two pairs of slip-on shoes on the floor—one pair for your mother and one pair for your father. You're going to place them facing in the direction you imagine your parents to be standing in when they were stuck in a recurring dynamic—however that dynamic played out. Using your intuition, hold each pair of shoes in your hands, one pair at a time, and let the shoes guide you to where they want to be placed in the room. Don't think about it; feel it. However you're guided to place the shoes is perfect.

Are your parents standing near each other? Are they facing each other? Are they facing away from each other? Does one look at the other while the other looks away? With their shoes on the floor, you are recreating the dynamic between them when you were a young child.

Now back away from the footprints and observe the dynamic. What's the first feeling that comes to you about their relationship? What's the overarching emotion you imagine they felt for each other? Do you feel their connection or disconnection? Did one want to be with the other more? Did one parent feel trapped in the relationship? Did both feel trapped? Was love flowing between them, or was the feeling more like apathy? Was there a coldness or bitterness between them? Can you feel their desire for each other, or was the energy more platonic?

If you're not sure, step into the shoes, one pair at a time. Clear your mind of any preconceived notions, and just feel the energy. Don't think about it. Just feel it. Stand in each pair as though you *are* them, and experience what they experienced. Stand first in one pair. Observe what you feel. Then stand in the other pair. Again, observe what you feel.

Use the space below to write down your observations. Keep writing until you've captured the entire experience.

....
....
....
....
....
....
....
....
....
....

Now envision your current or most recent intimate relationship. Is the energy similar? Have you recreated a similar dynamic? Which parent's emotion do you feel in your relationship? Which parent's suffering is still alive in you?

If you find yourself reliving a similar dynamic, face your parents' footprints and say these words.

"Mom, Dad, I've unconsciously recreated aspects of your relationship in mine. I often find myself [unhappy, or distant, or disconnected, or _____] with my partner, just like you were with each other. And I don't want to do this anymore. You had your turn. Now it's my turn, and I plan to give it my all. Please support me when I do it differently than you. Please bless me to be happy with my partner, even though you weren't happy with yours."

Use the space below to write down any new observations.

....
....
....
....
....

CHAPTER 12

MAXIMIZING YOUR SUCCESS

Many self-help books promise us financial success and fulfillment if only we follow the author's prescribed plan. Strategies such as developing effective habits, expanding our social network, visualizing our future success, and repeating money mantras are touted as ways to prosper. But what about those of us who never seem to achieve our goals no matter what we do or which plan we follow?

When our attempts at success repeatedly seem to collide with roadblocks and dead ends, it may be important to explore our family history. Unresolved traumatic events in our family can hinder how success flows to us and how well we are able to receive it. Dynamics ranging from sharing an unconscious identification with someone in the family who failed or was cheated or cheated someone, to receiving an undeserved inheritance, to experiencing the trauma of an early separation from a mother can all affect our ability to feel secure and financially vital.

EXERCISE

CONNECTING YOUR CORE LANGUAGE MAP TO YOUR SUCCESS

How would you define success? What does being successful mean to you?

....
....
....

Now answer this: How are you not successful? Or better yet, what do you think stands in the way of your success?

....
....
....

What's your worst fear about being successful? What's the worst thing that could happen to you if you had what you want?

....

....

....

Can you think of any events in your family history or early childhood that may be hindering your success?

....

....

....

FAMILY DYNAMICS THAT CAN LIMIT SUCCESS

Here are some of the main dynamics that can affect our relationship with success. Each acts as a silent force that can derail any forward progress we attempt to make.

Rejecting a Parent. Regardless of the story we tell about our parents, how good or bad they were, how hurt we feel by what they did or didn't do—when we reject them, we can limit our opportunities.

Our relationship with our parents is, in many ways, a metaphor for life. Those who feel that they received a lot from their parents often feel that they receive a lot from life. Feeling that we got only a small amount from our parents can translate into the feeling that we get only a small amount from life. Shortchanged by our parents, we can feel shortchanged by life.

When we feel disconnected from our mother, for example, we can unconsciously disconnect ourselves from the comforts of life. Security, safety, nurturance, care—all the elements associated with mothering—can feel missing in our lives. No matter how much we have, it can feel like we never have enough.

I often teach that an infant's wealth is a mother's focused attention. When her attention is steadfast, the infant feels ecstatic and abundant. When her attention is inconsistent or disengaged, the infant experiences a form of emotional bankruptcy. Not getting enough from our mother can create a blueprint for how much we let ourselves receive later in life.

The effects of rejecting a father can be equally limiting. A man, for instance, who rejects his father can experience himself as uncomfortable, self-conscious, or doubting himself in the company of other men. He can even find himself hesitant or reluctant to embrace the responsibilities associated with being a father—regardless of whether or not his father was the family provider or the family failure.

Unfinished business with either parent can cloud our work life as well as our social life. By unconsciously replaying unresolved family dynamics, we're likely to create conflicts instead of authentic connections. With old projections aimed at our bosses or coworkers, it can be difficult to flourish.

Repeating Our Rejected Parent's Life Experience. When we reject a parent, a strange symmetry linking us can occur; we can unwittingly walk in his or her shoes. What we judge as unacceptable or intolerable in our parent may reappear in our life. It can feel like an unwelcome inheritance.

We assume the opposite is true: the more we distance ourselves from our parents, the less likely we are to live similar lives and repeat their challenges. However, the converse appears to be truer. When we distance ourselves from them, we tend to become more like them and often lead lives similar to theirs.

If, for example, our father is rejected for being an alcoholic or a failure, we might drink or fail just like him.

An Unconscious Loyalty to Failure. We don't need to reject our parents to repeat their misfortunes. Sometimes we share an unconscious bond that keeps us mired in a similar experience. Despite our best efforts to succeed, we can find ourselves unable to achieve more in our lives than they achieved in theirs. If, for example, our father failed in business and wasn't able to provide financially for the family, we might unconsciously join him by failing in the same way. Ensnared in a hidden loyalty, we might sabotage our success, making sure that we don't surpass him.

The Legacy of Unfinished Business. Often, when a beloved member of the family dies early and is perceived not to have completed his or her life, someone later in the family, in silent collusion, can fail to complete something of great importance. The later family member can stop short of accomplishing a major task such as finishing a degree or closing a deal. Procrastination can also stem from being connected to a family member's early death.

While we can live unrecognized or unseen, like a family member who dies early, we can also live restricted or limited out of loyalty to a family member with a mental, physical, or emotional challenge by unconsciously sabotaging our own achievements.

Past Poverty Can Limit Present Prosperity. Sometimes we share an unconscious allegiance with ancestors who lived in poverty and had difficulty providing for themselves and their children. If our ancestors experienced great hardship, such as war, famine, persecution, slavery, or being forced to leave their homeland, we can continue their suffering without realizing it, and thwart our attempts at living an abundant life. It can be difficult to have more than they had.

Often, a simple ritual that honors our family members who struggled grounds us so that we can take advantage of the "new" life we received from their efforts.

Personal Guilt Can Suppress Success. Sometimes we have personally taken advantage of people or hurt them in a way that has created significant suffering. Maybe we acquired an undeserved sum of money through manipulation or subterfuge, such as by marrying for wealth or embezzling from the company we work for. When such an event takes place, we often cannot hold on to this financial gain. Regardless of whether we feel guilty or not, or whether we consider the consequences of our actions or not, we and/or our children can live meager lives to balance the harm we've done.

All in all, the consequences of our actions, the effects of unresolved family traumas, our relationship with our parents, and entanglements with members of our family system who suffered can all be obstacles that stand in the way of our success. Once we make the link to the past and integrate what remains out of balance in the present, we've taken a crucial step. When everyone and everything is held with respectful consideration, the unfinished business from the past can remain in the past, and we can move forward with more freedom and financial ease.

EXERCISE

WHAT'S BLOCKING YOUR SUCCESS?

To explore the ways these family dynamics may have limited your success, consider the following statements. Check any that apply, and write down your thoughts, feelings, memories, or stories on the lines below.

The Success Checklist

☐ had a challenging relationship with my mother.

☐ I had a challenging relationship with my father.

☐ My father or mother wasn't successful in his or her career.

☐ My father or mother failed in providing for the family.

☐ My parents separated when I was young.

☐ My mother was unhappy with my father.

☐ My father was unhappy with my mother.

☐ I experienced a physical or emotional separation from my

- mother when I was young.
- [ ] My mother or father died young.
- [ ] My grandparent died young.
- [ ] One of my parents or grandparents had a sibling who died young.
- [ ] I gained significantly at someone else's expense.
- [ ] Someone in my family gained significantly at someone else's expense.
- [ ] Someone in my family was cheated out of an inheritance.
- [ ] Someone in my family inherited or acquired wealth unjustly.
- [ ] Someone in my family went bankrupt, lost the family wealth, or caused the family to experience financial difficulty.
- [ ] Someone outside my family caused my family to experience financial difficulty.
- [ ] Someone in my family was rejected for being a failure, a loser, a gambler, et cetera.
- [ ] Someone in my family lost a home or possessions and had difficulty recovering.
- [ ] I had impoverished ancestors.
- [ ] I emigrated from my country.
- [ ] My parents emigrated from their country.
- [ ] My family members were forced to flee or were driven out of their homeland.
- [ ] I hurt, cheated, or took advantage of someone.
- [ ] Someone in my family hurt, cheated, or took advantage of someone.

Connecting the dots, which of the above experiences may be related to your personal challenges with success? List them here.

....

....

....

Now, let's go a step further and bring in the four unconscious themes. The following practice can help deepen your understanding of what might be limiting your success and, at the same time, help set you free.

PRACTICE

SUCCESS AND THE FOUR UNCONSCIOUS THEMES

Look at the boxes you checked in The Success Checklist one more time. Can you tell which one or more of the four unconscious themes has been silently operating in the background?

- ▶ Has a break in the bond with your mother limited your relationship with abundance?
- ▶ Have you merged with a parent who failed or suffered in some way?

- Have you rejected a parent and feel cut off from success?

- Have you identified with a family member who took advantage of someone, lived in poverty, suffered, or failed, et cetera?

Which unconscious theme may be limiting your success?

UNCONSCIOUS THEME	HOW IT HAS AFFECTED MY SUCCESS
MERGED WITH A PARENT	
REJECTED A PARENT	
BREAK IN THE BOND	
IDENTIFIED WITH FAMILY MEMBER(S)	

REMOVING OUR BARRIER TO SUCCESS

Place two pairs of slip-on shoes on the floor—one for you and one for the person who may be impeding your success. This could be someone in your family system you've identified with, or a parent you've merged with. (This pair of shoes can also represent multiple people, such as your impoverished ancestors, or both the cheater and the one who was cheated, etc.)

Now stand in the second pair of shoes as though you *are* that person (or those people). Experience what that person (or those people) must have felt. Do you feel anger? Frustration? Worthlessness? Hopelessness? Shame? Agony? Despair?

Use the space below to write down your observations.

....
....
....

Now go back and stand in your own shoes. Tell this person or those people: "I see I've been unconsciously connected to you. It's been affecting what I have and what I'm able to hold on to. Today, I rewrite the contract between us. I leave all suffering in the past where it belongs. From now on, I'll enjoy what is mine by living fully in my abundance and relishing the rewards I earn."

Use the space below to further explore the dynamic that's been limiting your abundance. Have you been connected to a family member who failed? Did someone in your family cheat another, or was cheated, and it's been a challenge to hold on to what you have? Did you have a break in the bond with your mother that keeps you feeling like you never have enough, no matter how much you have? Whatever the dynamic, keep writing until your insights are clear.

....
....
....
....
....

Now, write down some words or sentences that you can imagine saying to this person (or these people) to break your entanglement.

....
....
....
....
....

CHAPTER 13

EXPANDING YOUR LIFE FORCE

At this point in the workbook, you're likely standing in a different place with a new perspective. Maybe you feel lighter inside. With your core sentence and your core language map, you've already begun to disentangle from the web of inherited fear. What once functioned as an unconscious mantra that kept you rooted in suffering can now be a resource that sets you free.

Even though this workbook lays out multiple strategies for healing, ultimately there's really nothing to fix. The spirit of who we are, the spark of our existence, already exists within. Yet for many of us, our focus has become trying to heal something we believe is terribly wrong with us. We strive to be more conscious, more present, more successful. Perhaps a true measure of healing is when we no longer feel the need to be anything other than who we are. Instead, we simply live our lives.

Having said that, I've included some practices in this chapter to keep that spark vibrant. These practices are simple but powerful. I find that people who heal from trauma don't attach to the outcome of a practice. They don't say: "I'm doing this just so my headaches go away." They do the practice because the practice feels right in their body. They embrace the process without knowing exactly where it will lead.

 **PRACTICE**

REVISITING KEY PRACTICES

Sift through the pages of this workbook again, and mark the practices, exercises, rituals, and healing sentences that had the biggest impact. Remember, each time you repeat a healing practice, you create new neural pathways in your brain and new experiences in your body. Just by soaking in the sensations of new experiences, you ground and deepen your healing.

Which healing sentences and practices did you find most helpful?

....

....

....

Which practices can you envision returning to when old fears arise?

....

....

....

PRACTICE

WHEN OLD FEARS ARISE

Remaining in the good feelings isn't always easy. We can begin our "positive feeling" practice, and then quickly sink back into our old, familiar negative thoughts. *This practice may work for other people, but it won't work for me. Nothing works for me. No matter how hard I try, I never seem to get better.*

Thoughts like these are normal. Remember what we learned earlier. Our amygdala locks onto negative thoughts and feelings believing, by doing so, it's protecting us from harm. Replaying painful feelings and recogitating worrisome thoughts is its unconscious strategy to protect us. It's almost as if an unconscious voice is saying: *If I keep myself down, I'm less likely to be kicked down.* This strategy, as we know, though it's common to many of us, doesn't protect us. It actually does the opposite. It keeps us clenched in a state of fight, flight, freeze, and blocks the good feelings from arising.

If you find the old fears or feelings returning, follow these three simple steps:

Recognize the familiar fears and feelings inside you. If they're not clear, you might try saying your old core sentence aloud or silently to yourself. As you feel the words, allow the sensations of the old fear to arise, just for a moment, so that you can become familiar with the feelings. These sensations can signal that the switch of your core sentence has been turned on without your knowledge.

Acknowledge that the old fear has become activated. Once you become aware of it, you have the power to break its hold.

Take an action to separate from the spiraling feelings. The action you take is important. You might start by telling yourself: "These are not my feelings. I've merely inherited them from my family." Sometimes, acknowledging this is enough. You might also envision the traumatic event that once held you captive, or the family member with whom you've been identified. As you do so, remind yourself that these feelings have now been laid to rest and that the family members involved now comfort and support you.

You might also consider placing your hand on your body where you notice the old feelings and breathe deeply, allowing your exhale to lengthen inside you. As you do this, you might even ask yourself: What new experience am I noticing in my body at this very moment? When you direct your focus and your breath into your body and feel the sensations that reside there, without letting yourself become triggered by them, you can shift your inner experience.

Let the sensations of these positive experiences affect you physically, viscerally, to the point where you come to know them and trust the feeling of them in your body.

By following these steps, you calm the brain's trauma response and enrich the parts of the brain that can help you feel better. With repetition and focused attention, the new thoughts, images, emotions, and feelings will remain, stabilizing you through the ups and downs of everyday life.

Traumas may be challenging, but they also give us a pathway for growth. Generally, we don't become great without surmounting something great. In that respect, as we navigate the difficult waters of trauma, learning how to survive, we're also developing powerful strategies that make us successful. And we'll have multiple opportunities to continue that success. As Freud reminds us, a trauma, seeking a positive resolution, will keep repeating. The contraction, ultimately seeking its expansion, will repeat until that expansion happens.

Here's a practice to feel that expansion now.

PRACTICE

STEPPING FULLY INTO THE FUTURE WHILE HONORING THE PAST

Find six pairs of shoes to represent your mother, your mother's parents, your father, and your father's parents. Place the shoes behind you, so that your father's shoes are just behind your right shoulder, and your mother's shoes are just behind your left shoulder. Then place their parents' shoes behind them, with their mother's shoes on the left and their father's shoes on their right.

With your parents and grandparents at your back, step into your own shoes and feel their support, as though it were a current of energy flowing from them to you. Take a minute and let yourself soak this energy in. Feel it soaking into your cells. Feel yourself receiving their support and blessing to live a long, healthy life, a life that's full and joyous.

Now say the following words to them:

"Thank you for all you've given me. To honor you, and all that you've gone through, I promise to live a good life, a loving life. Even if things were difficult between us, I'll take the gift of my life and make something good out of it. I'll honor you by living the best life I can."

Feel your words being received. Now, for a silent minute, let something pass forward from them to you. You don't have to know what it is. Just feel it. It may be a physical feeling, or a message, or a wave of well-being moving through you. Whatever it is, just receive it.

Write down what you experienced. Keep writing until you've captured all of it.

....
....
....

....
....
....
....
....
....
....

PRACTICE

STANDING IN YOUR OWN FOOTSTEPS

There's just one more thing I'd like to ask you to do.

Take your pair of slip-on shoes and place them in front of your favorite window, where you have a view of nature or something life-giving—kids playing on the grass, birds singing in a tree, the sun peeking out from over a hill—whatever image you find inspiring or fills your heart.

Step into the shoes and feel the new you, rich with wisdom and experience. Feel yourself taking your rightful place in life. How does it feel to ground in your own energy, unencumbered by the influences of the past? How does it feel to draw up your own life force into your body? How does it feel to finally have your own space?

Send your breath into that space, where it lives in your body. The more you feel it, the more of it there is. Let the sensations arise, and just breathe into them. Expand them inward with your inhalation and outward with your exhalation. Follow the sensations with your awareness. Imagine you're riding on top of them, letting them lead you on a sensory journey. Ride them until you become them, until you merge with them. Ride them, if you're willing, until there's no you anymore. No mind. No thoughts. Just life force expanding throughout your core. This journey is the true journey home to yourself.

Write down what you feel. Keep writing until you've captured the whole experience.

....
....
....
....
....
....
....
....
....
....

Some final words: I want to thank you for venturing with me through the pages of this workbook. Weaving through the shadows of family history isn't always easy, but you made it. The journey of transformation cannot be underestimated. I want to acknowledge what you just did and emphasize the importance of this work. When we do this work, we not only elevate ourselves, we elevate our relationships, our families, our communities, and most importantly, we add to the collective peace of humanity as a whole. I want to personally thank you for that. My greatest wish is that you become the expansion of life force that allows you to live fully and love deeply.

MARK WOLYNN

GLOSSARY

Bridging Question: A question that can connect a persistent symptom, issue, or fear to a core trauma or to a family member who struggled similarly.

Core Complaint: Our main issue, whether internalized or projected outward, which is often derived from fragments of traumatic experience and expressed in core language.

Core Descriptors: Adjectives and short descriptive phrases that reveal the unconscious feelings we hold toward our parents.

Core Language: The idiosyncratic words and sentences of our deepest fears that provide clues leading to the source of an unresolved trauma. Core language can also be expressed in physical sensations, behaviors, emotions, impulses, and symptoms of an illness or condition.

Core Sentence: A short sentence that expresses the emotionally charged language of our deepest fear. It carries the residue of an unresolved trauma from our early childhood or family history.

Core Trauma: The unresolved trauma in our early or family history that can unconsciously affect our behaviors, choices, health, and well-being.

Genogram: A two-dimensional visual representation of a family tree.

Healing Sentence: A sentence of reconciliation or resolution that brings about new images and feelings of well-being.

ACKNOWLEDGMENTS

A number of people unselfishly shared their time and talents making this workbook possible. I'm humbled and blessed by the kindness and generosity they showed me.

First, I'm deeply grateful to my friend, the gifted writer Amanda Rooker. Insisting she gain visceral understanding of the work, she immersed herself into its depths. Then, with a thoughtful hand and gentle heart, she helped me sculpt this workbook into a seamless experience, adding essential nuggets along the way. Her intelligence can be felt throughout these pages.

Dr. Shannon Zaychuk spent countless hours working and reworking the early drafts of *It Didn't Start with You* with me. From conceptualizing to shaping words on the page, she helped forge the foundation on which this workbook is built. Her expertise and pivotal insights added a profound dimension to this work.

I'm also grateful to my research assistant Katarina Baltayan-Pautz for her no-nonsense intelligence, her fine-tuned ear for language and meaning, her keen ability to mind-meld with me, enabling us to think as one, and the numerous hours she dedicated to this project. Her help was instrumental.

Bonnie Solow, agent extraordinaire—I'm grateful for your friendship, for you recognizing the importance of my work, for your discerning wisdom, and for your impeccable guidance.

I feel lucky to have worked directly with the vice president and publisher of Penguin, Patrick Nolan. I'm extremely appreciative of his editorial savvy, his genuine kindness, his creative mind, and his encouragement every step of the way.

I'd also like to thank the president and publisher of Penguin, Brian Tart, for his trust in me and his support to summon my newest work to the written page. And to Emma Dollar and the entire team at Penguin—a huge thank you.

Dr. Isabelle Mansuy, professor in neuroepigenetics in the medical faculty of the University of Zurich, took time to share her knowledge with me. I'm appreciative of that and for her pioneering insights about transgenerational epigenetic inheritance that appear throughout this workbook.

Anna Catarina, my life partner—your help was incalculable. Your extraordinary mind, keen suggestions, infinite support, and the countless matcha lattes you brewed for me kept me going late into the night.

I am enormously grateful to all my teachers, especially the late Dr. Roger Woolger, who also shared a love of language. Roger helped me decode the urgent language of the unconscious. His work deeply inspired my own. I also want to acknowledge the late Jeru Kabbal, who helped me, with adversity present, to stay present.

Beyond any words that can be written here, I am profoundly grateful to the late Bert Hellinger for being my teacher and supporting me in my work. What he has given me is immeasurable.

Lastly, I am indebted to all the courageous people who shared their stories with me. My deepest hope is that I have honored them in these pages.

NOTES

INTRODUCTION: DO YOU HAVE INHERITED FAMILY TRAUMA?

1. Names and identifying characteristics have been changed.

CHAPTER 1: HOW WE INHERIT THE EFFECTS OF TRAUMA

1. Caleb E. Finch and John C. Loehlin, "Environmental Influences That May Precede Fertilization: A First Examination of the Prezygotic Hypothesis from Maternal Age Influences on Twins," *Behavioral Genetics* 28, no. 2 (1998): 101, doi.org/10.1023/A:1021415823234.
2. Thomas W. Sadler, *Langman's Medical Embryology*, 9th ed. (Lippincott Williams & Wilkins, 2009), 13.
3. Tracy Bale, "Epigenetic and Transgenerational Reprogramming of Brain Development," *Nature Reviews Neuroscience* 16 (2015): 332–44, doi.org/10.1038/nrn3818.

4. For an in-depth review of this research, see Mark Wolynn, *It Didn't Start with You: How Inherited Family Trauma Shapes Who We Are and How to End the Cycle*, rev. ed. (Penguin, 2025).
5. Interview with Mark Wolynn, February 7, 2024.
6. Patrick McGowan et al., "The Legacy of Child Abuse," *Headway* 4, no. 1 (2009), McGill University.
7. Jamie Hackett, "Scientists Discover How Epigenetic Information Could Be Inherited," University of Cambridge, January 25, 2013, cam.ac.uk/research/news/scientists-discover-how-epigenetic-information-could-be-inherited.
8. To learn more about the research behind inherited family trauma, see Wolynn, *It Didn't Start with You*, rev. ed.
9. Natalie Rahhal, "Men Who Suffered Trauma as Children May Pass On Their Anxiety to Their Kids Through Their Sperm, Study Finds," *Daily Mail*, May 22, 2018, dailymail.co.uk/health/article-5759347/Men-suffered-trauma-children-pass-anxiety-kids-sperm.html. For the original study, see David A. Dickson et al., "Reduced Levels of miRNAs 449 and 34 in Sperm of Mice and Men Exposed to Early Life Stress," *Translational Psychiatry* 8, no. 101 (2018), doi.org/10.1038/s41398-018-0146-2.
10. Jef Akst, "Transgenerational Trauma Passed Down from WWII Evacuees," *The Scientist*, November 29, 2017, the-scientist.com/transgenerational-trauma-passed-down-from-wwii-evacuees-30571. For the original study, see Torsten Santavirta et al., "Association of the World War II Finnish Evacuation of Children with Psychiatric Hospitalization in the Next Generation," *JAMA Psychiatry* 75, no. 1 (2018): 21–27, doi.org/10.1001/jamapsychiatry.2017.3511.
11. Studies with worms have shown epigenetic changes could be traced up to three hundred generations: "Match Matters: The Right Combination of Parents Can Turn a Gene Off Indefinitely," ScienceDaily, July 9, 2021, sciencedaily.com/releases/2021/07/210709094505.htm. For the original study, see Sindhuja Devanapally et al., "Mating Can Initiate Stable RNA Silencing That Overcomes Epigen-

etic Recovery," *Nature Communications* 12, no. 1 (2021), doi.org/10.1038/s41467-021-24053-4. Also, in studies with stickleback fish, researchers discovered sons and daughters experienced different reactions to their parents' traumas, with predator-exposed fathers producing riskier, bolder behaviors in sons but not in daughters, and predator-exposed mothers producing anxiety in both sons and daughters. See Jennifer Hellmann, "In Fish, Parents' Stressful Experiences Influence Offspring Behavior via Epigenetic Changes," *The Conversation*, March 30, 2021, theconversation.com/in-fish-parents-stressful-experiences-influence-offspring-behavior-via-epigenetic-changes-156833.

CHAPTER 2: A BREAK IN THE BOND

1. Reference from Mark Wolynn, *It Didn't Start with You: How Inherited Family Trauma Shapes Who We Are and How to End the Cycle*, rev. ed. (Penguin, 2025).
2. Dylan G. Gee and Emily M. Cohodes, "Influences of Caregiving on Development: A Sensitive Period for Biological Embedding of Predictability and Safety Cues," *Current Directions in Psychological Science* 30, no. 5 (2021): 376–83, doi.org/10.1177/09637214211015673.
3. Winifred Gallagher, "Motherless Child," *The Sciences* 32, no. 4 (1992): 12–15, esp. 13, doi.org/10.1002/j.2326-1951.1992.tb02399.x.
4. Raylene Phillips, "The Sacred Hour: Uninterrupted Skin-to-Skin Contact Immediately After Birth," *Newborn & Infant Nursing Reviews* 13, no. 2 (2013): 67–72, doi.org/10.1053/j.nainr.2013.04.001.
5. Edward Tronick and Andrew Gianino, "Interactive Mismatch and Repair: Challenges to the Coping Infant," *Zero to Three* 6, no. 3 (1986): 1–6; Donald Winnicott, *Babies and Their Mothers* (Perseus, 1987).

6. Edward Tronick and Marjorie Beeghly, "Infants' Meaning-Making and the Development of Mental Health Problems," *American Psychologist* 66, no. 2 (2011): 107–19, doi.org/10.1037/a0021631.

CHAPTER 8: FROM INSIGHT TO INTEGRATION

1. Andrew Newberg and Mark Robert Waldman, *Words Can Change Your Brain* (Penguin, 2012), 3.
2. Newberg and Waldman, *Words Can Change Your Brain*, 35.
3. David Samuels, "Do Jews Carry Trauma in Our Genes? A Conversation with Rachel Yehuda," Tablet, December 11, 2014, https://images.shulcloud.com/4182/uploads/Archives/DoJewsCarryTraumainTheirGenes.pdf.
4. Rick Hanson, "How to Trick Your Brain for Happiness," *Greater Good Magazine*, September 26, 2011, greatergood.berkeley.edu/article/item/how_to_trick_your_brain_for_happiness.